*Sunset*

# Fireplaces & Wood Stoves

*By the Editors of Sunset Books and Sunset Magazine*

*Warming wood stove (also shown on page 64).*

## Lane Publishing Co. ▪ Menlo Park, California

*See-through fireplace invites fireside reading (also shown on page 24).*

Book Editor
**Fran Feldman**

Contributing Editors
**Michael Bowker**
**Barbara J. Braasch**

Coordinating Editor
**Gregory J. Kaufman**

Design
**Joe di Chiarro**

Illustrations
**Mark Pechenik**

# Warm Comfort

Today's fireplaces and wood stoves are considerably more heat-efficient— and, in the case of wood stoves, cleaner burning—than their predecessors. In addition to warming your home, they also provide a natural gathering place for family and friends as they relax in the warmth and glow of the fire.

Whether you're planning to build a dramatic masonry fireplace in your living room or you're shopping for a wood stove that will be your home's only source of heat, this book will help you every step of the way. The first chapter describes how the various types of fireplaces and wood stoves work. Next, you'll discover an exciting array of photographs that will give you hundreds of design ideas. The planning, installation, and maintenance information that follows will guide you through the process of buying, installing, and using your fireplace or wood stove.

We are especially grateful to the following energy consultants and experts for their help with the preparation of this book: Karen and Jay Fenton of Energy Unlimited; Bruno Freschet; Rich Nichols and Kelly Whalen of Placerville Energy Center; George Pliant of the Wood Energy Institute West; Earl Prunty of Prunty Masonry; Bob Pyne of Hearth and Home; and Mell Rottiers and Matt Stewart of The Golden Flame.

We also want to thank Anchor Fireplace; Clervi Marble Company; Country Flame; John Crouch and Gary Satterfield of the Wood Heating Alliance; Linda Derosier of Dovre, Inc.; Emerald Homes; Fox Glen; Jotul USA, Inc.; Malm Fireplaces; Daniel Melcon; Okell's Fireplace of San Francisco; Osburn Manufacturing; Pacwest Development; Ruegg Fireplaces; and Vermont Castings.

**Photographers:** Russell Abraham: 33 bottom; Anchor Fireplace: 15, 28 top; Dovre, Inc.: 42 right; Glenn Christiansen: 24 bottom, 31 left, 40; Peter Christiansen: 4, 27 top left and top right, 29 top; Country Flame: 50 right; Philip Harvey: 19 top, 29 bottom, 32, 34 top, 37 top, 45 bottom, 49 right, 51 right, 56; William Helsel: 2, 24 top; Jotul USA, Inc.: 50 left, 53 bottom, 55 bottom; Jack McDowell: 20 left, 21, 25; Stephen Marley: 16 top, 18, 20 right, 22 top, 23, 31 right, 35, 36, 38 top, 41 top, 63 top; Osburn Manufacturing: 51 left; Jim Peck: 30 right; Norman A. Plate: 19 bottom, 30 left; Ruegg Fireplaces: 22 bottom; Chad Slattery: 27 bottom, 39; Tom Wyatt: 1, 8 right and left, 12, 14, 16 bottom, 17 top and bottom, 26, 28 bottom, 33 top, 34 bottom, 37 bottom, 38 bottom left, center, and right, 41 bottom, 42 left, 43 top and bottom, 44, 45 top, 46 top and bottom, 47 top and bottom, 48, 49 left, 52 top and bottom, 53 top, 54, 55 top, 59, 62, 63 bottom, 64.

**Photo stylist:** JoAnn Masaoka Van Atta: 1, 8 right and left, 12, 14, 16 bottom, 17 top, 19 top, 23, 28, 29 bottom, 32, 34 top and bottom, 36, 37 top, 38 bottom, 41 bottom, 42 left, 43 top and bottom, 45 bottom, 46 top and bottom, 47 top and bottom, 49 right, 51 right, 52 top and bottom, 53 top, 55 top and bottom, 56, 59, 62, 63 top and bottom, 64.

**Cover:** Heat-circulating fireplace, handsomely framed with marble, warms wood-paneled library/sitting area. Fireplace heats by convection: cool air enters through vents below firebox, warmed air is expelled above. Architect: L. Allen Sayles. Cover design by Susan Bryant. Photography by Tom Wyatt. Photo styling by JoAnn Masaoka Van Atta.

Editor, Sunset Books: Elizabeth L. Hogan

First printing October 1989

# CONTENTS

## Special Features

# FIREPLACES & WOOD STOVES– THE BASICS

*In the widening search for alternatives to scarce and expensive fuels in home heating, a growing number of home owners are discovering the advantages of heating with wood. Old in concept yet modern in application, fireplaces and wood stoves, designed for efficiency and used correctly, can spread their warmth over your home.*

*But fireplaces and wood stoves can do much more than just heat your house. A focal point for gatherings of family and friends alike, a fireplace or wood stove draws guests within its glowing circle, evoking dozens, if not hundreds, of pleasing associations. Your fireplace or wood stove may take center stage in your home by virtue of its design and location. Often, it expresses your style of living, whether it be formal or casual.*

*Although much of the enjoyment of having a fireplace or wood stove rests with its social warmth, more and more attention is now being focused on heat efficiency. Using new materials and designs, manufacturers have developed products that do a much better job of heating your house than was ever possible in the past. An understanding of how the different fireplaces and wood stoves work will help you make the right choice for your situation.*

## HOW FIREPLACES & WOOD STOVES HEAT

Fireplaces and wood stoves heat in two different ways: by radiation and by convection. The type of heater you have determines in large part its heating effectiveness.

■ *Radiation* is the direct transmission of energy in the form of infrared rays; these rays will heat objects they strike, although they don't contribute to heating the air space in between.

Radiant fireplaces, the traditional fireplace type without any air vents, are inefficient as producers of usable heat. What heat is produced comes mainly from the firebox opening, but only about 10 percent of the heat generated in the firebox is emitted into the room. The other 90 percent goes up the chimney.

Moreover, open-hearth radiant fireplaces gulp large quantities of air, causing interior drafts. In some cases, they can actually decrease the temperature of a room by pulling in air from outside the house.

Radiant wood stoves, on the other hand, can be very effective heaters because of the amount of heat that's conducted through the metal walls of the stove (see page 11).

■ *Convection* is the movement of heat through air or fluids. When air is heated, it rises, setting up convective currents that circulate air.

Convective fireplaces, which circulate heated air back into the room, usually through vents above the firebox, give off as much heat as radiant types, but to this they add circulating air warmed by convection.

*Wall cutout frames concrete and polished galvanized-steel fireplace, sculptural focal point for living room. Architect: Jerry Lee, LDA Architects.*

These fireplaces, often referred to as heat-circulating, generally have a double- or triple-wall firebox with an intervening air space several inches wide. Ducts draw cool air into this space, where the air is warmed and expelled by convection through vents above the firebox opening, as shown in the illustration below.

Some new fireplace designs include small fans that drive the heated air from the fireplace through ducts to other rooms of the house.

Convective stoves are also efficient heaters; they utilize air currents to spread heat throughout the room or to other rooms. This is usually accomplished by an air passage, or envelope, between the firebox and the outer metal wall. The cool air from the intake travels through the passage, where it's warmed and passed out the top or sides of the stove. (For more information on convective wood stoves, see page 12.)

## Heat-circulating Fireplace

*In heat-circulating fireplace, cool air is warmed in air space around firebox and then vented into room.*

## A VARIETY OF FIREPLACES

The only real warmth generated by the majority of fireplaces is their appearance. The traditional open-hearth radiant fireplace provides about as much heat as did the open fires of prehistoric man.

But today's demand for more heat-efficient fireplaces has resulted in new designs that can increase the efficiency even of radiant fireplaces. Inside a typical-looking masonry fireplace, for example, can lurk a modular masonry mass that stores heat for release later on, making the fireplace far more efficient than the conventional type.

Another design change that increases heating efficiency is the addition of ceramic or tempered glass doors to the front of the fireplace. These help control the amount of air being pulled into the fireplace, eliminating interior room drafts. Doors are available for all types of fireplaces; in some areas, building codes require that all factory-built fireplaces be fitted with them.

Masonry, including high-mass modular, and factory-built are the two most common fireplaces. Other popular types include hybrid, freestanding, and gas fireplaces. All are described below. For information on installing a fireplace, turn to page 73.

## MASONRY FIREPLACES

Although traditionally thought of as brick fireplaces, these fireplaces can be made of other masonry materials as well. Masonry styles come in both radiant and convection designs. Although difficult and costly to build, they're very durable and lend a certain ambience to a home.

Because of their substantial weight —most of them weigh about 5,000 pounds—masonry fireplaces are usually found on the ground floor and are built on an outside wall.

Most masonry fireplaces have a solid firebox leading upward to a damper, smoke shelf, smoke dome, and chimney. (The anatomy of a typical masonry fireplace is illustrated on the facing page.) The chimney itself is also made from masonry.

When convective principles (see page 5) are applied to a conventional fireplace, heating efficiency is substantially improved, as it is with a high-mass modular fireplace.

Patterned after Northern European stove designs, high-mass modular fireplaces have relatively small fireboxes, as shown on page 8. A labyrinth of precast masonry components containing heat-exchange chambers extends above the firebox, capturing and storing heat from the escaping smoke as it exits the chimney. The masonry mass then gradually and steadily releases the heat into the room.

Most modular units have a controlled-combustion design, and some utilize ductwork to disperse the captured heat. Some of these units have been found to be four times more heat efficient than conventional fireplaces.

Special structural support is required for the 300- to 600-pound fire-

## Anatomy of a Conventional Fireplace

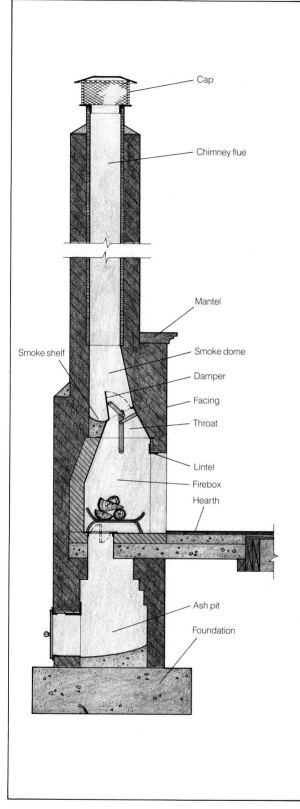

*Conventional masonry fireplace rests on a reinforced concrete foundation. Many fireplaces today omit ash pit below firebox. Cap at top of chimney may not be required in all areas.*

### Cap

The cap prevents foreign objects from entering the chimney. An integral spark arrester protects against sparks.

### Chimney flue

Smoke and combustion gases from the burning wood pass up the chimney inside a flue, usually made of large-diameter terra cotta pipe or insulated stainless steel.

### Mantel

Usually made of wood, the mantel is a shelf above the firebox opening used for decorative purposes.

### Smoke dome

The smoke dome acts as a funnel to compress smoke and gases rising from the fire so they'll squeeze into the flue.

### Smoke shelf

The smoke shelf bounces stray down drafts back up the chimney before they can neutralize the updraft and blow smoke into the room.

### Damper

A steel or cast-iron door that opens or closes the throat opening, the damper is used to check and regulate draft, and prevents the loss of heat up the chimney.

### Facing

The vertical surface around the fireplace opening is called the facing. It can be made of various materials.

### Throat

An opening above the firebox, the throat is where flame, smoke, and combustion gases pass into the smoke chamber.

### Lintel

The lintel is a heavy steel brace that supports the masonry above the fireplace opening.

### Firebox

Made of steel or firebrick, the firebox is where the fire is built. The walls and back of the firebox are slightly slanted in order to radiate heat into the room.

### Hearth

The inner hearth of firebrick or steel holds the burning fuel; the outer hearth, which also must be made of noncombustible material, protects the floor from heat and sparks.

### Ash pit

Ashes are dumped through an opening in the hearth into the fireproof storage compartment below.

### Foundation

Usually a reinforced concrete slab, the foundation holds the weight of the masonry fireplace and chimney structures.

box and the additional 3,000 pounds of heat-storing mass.

## FACTORY-BUILT FIREPLACES

Factory-built fireplaces come in both radiant and heat-circulating designs. They have metal, as opposed to masonry, fireboxes; although they may not last as long as the masonry types, their record of durability is good.

You'll find factory-built fireplaces in dozens of different designs, from elaborate to very simple. Prices vary accordingly. All share the same basic advantages: relatively low cost, ease of installation, and freedom of location, thanks to their relatively light weight (600 to 800 pounds, including the facing). Moreover, units can be fitted either to masonry chimneys or to stovepipes.

Clearances to combustible walls and floors vary widely, depending on style; before you buy, be sure to note the manufacturer's specifications.

## Components of a Modular Fireplace

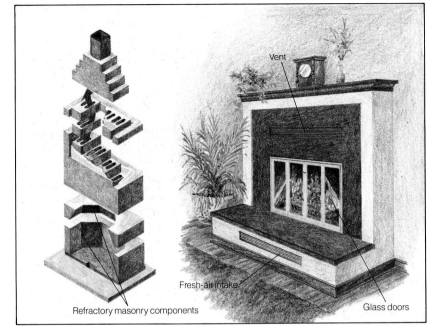

Vent

Refractory masonry components

Fresh-air intake

Glass doors

*Massive heat storage area (shown at left) inside this modular fireplace captures and stores heat from fire, then releases it over time. Room air is ducted directly to fire; heated air is vented out above firebox, as shown at right.*

## Factory-built Fireplace

*Marble facing and hearth adorn heat-circulating factory-built fireplace fitted with glass doors.*

## High-mass Modular Fireplace

*Within this modular fireplace, masonry components store heat, releasing it gradually into room.*

# WHICH WOOD TO BURN?

Burning wood for heat frees you from reliance on the power company or fuel truck; and when power outages or fuel shortages occur, it's comforting to know that a source of heat is as close as the wood pile.

Costwise, wood is definitely competitive with fossil fuels and electricity in most parts of the country. In fact, dwindling fossil fuel supplies and the development of more efficient wood stoves have made wood burning one of the cheapest ways to heat.

Not all species of wood are available everywhere. The kind of wood you'll burn will depend in large part on the species that grow in your area. (High transportation costs prevent firewood from being trucked very far.)

If you compare wood pound for pound, all wood of comparable sea-soning yields about the same amount of usable heat. However, wood is sold by the cord, not by the pound, and hardwoods weigh more than softwoods. As a result, a cord of hardwood is usually more expensive than a cord of softwood, but hardwoods yield much more usable heat.

The chart below provides a guide to the characteristics of the basic types of firewood. Instructions on cutting wood and on purchasing wood that's already been cut are on page 110.

| Type of wood | Amount of heat | Ease of burning | Smoke density | Pops or throws sparks | Ease of splitting |
|---|---|---|---|---|---|
| **Hardwoods:** | | | | | |
| Ash | High | Good | Low | No | Good |
| Aspen | Low | Good | Medium | No | Good |
| Basswood | Low | Good | Medium | No | Good |
| Beech | High | Good | Low | No | Good |
| Birch | High | Good | Low | No | Good |
| Cherry | Medium | Good | Low | No | Good |
| Cottonwood | Low | Good | Medium | No | Good |
| Elm | Medium | Medium | Medium | No | Poor |
| Eucalyptus | High | Good | Low | No | Good |
| Gum | Medium | Medium | Medium | No | Poor |
| Hickory | High | Good | Low | No | Good |
| Maples<br>　hard<br>　soft | <br>High<br>Medium | <br>Good<br>Good | <br>Low<br>Low | <br>No<br>No | <br>Good<br>Good |
| Oak | High | Good | Low | No | Good |
| Sycamore | Medium | Medium | Medium | No | Poor |
| Walnut | Medium | Good | Low | No | Good |
| **Softwoods:** | | | | | |
| Cedars (eastern, western, white) | Low | Good | Medium | Yes | Good |
| Douglas fir | Medium | Good | High | No | Medium |
| Larch | Medium | Good | Medium | No | Good |
| Pines<br>　eastern white<br>　Ponderosa<br>　southern yellow<br>　sugar<br>　western white | <br>Low<br>Low<br>Medium<br>Low<br>Low | <br>Medium<br>Medium<br>Good<br>Medium<br>Medium | <br>Medium<br>Medium<br>High<br>Medium<br>Medium | <br>No<br>No<br>No<br>No<br>No | <br>Medium<br>Good<br>Good<br>Medium<br>Medium |
| Spruce | Low | Good | Medium | Yes | Good |
| Tamarack | Medium | Good | Medium | Yes | Good |
| True firs | Low | Medium | Medium | Yes | Medium |

## Hybrid Fireplace

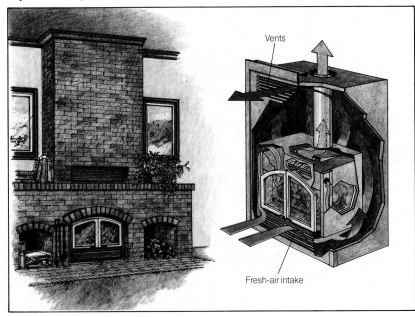

Vents

Fresh-air intake

allow them to burn at an efficiency level equal to that of many wood stoves.

Air-control designs allow the operator to control the amount of heat produced. Gasketed glass doors stop air leaks and interior drafts, yet provide the look of a traditional fireplace.

Hybrids (see illustration at left) cost more than factory-built fireplaces and other heat-circulating types but may pay for themselves over time through lower heating bills. Some special adaptations may be needed if you plan to retrofit a hybrid into an existing fireplace. Consult the manufacturer or dealer to see if special supports or clearances are necessary.

## FREESTANDING FIREPLACES

Because they radiate heat to all sides, freestanding fireplaces are fairly efficient heaters. One type of freestanding fireplace has a firepit in which the fire is open all around; smoke rises into a hood and then into a chimney. Another type is made from a prefabricated metal unit, which typically is shaped somewhere between a cylinder and a sphere and has an opening on one side.

Freestanding fireplaces work best if they're located so that heat can radiate

## HYBRID FIREPLACES

Hybrid fireplaces duplicate most of the heat-producing elements of wood stoves, including a sophisticated approach toward controlling combustion air, in a fireplace setting.

They're similar to wood stove inserts, but they have large glass doors, heat-exchange systems, and heat ducts that vent heated air back into the room, usually by natural convection but sometimes with the aid of small fans. Their sophisticated heat-exchange systems

# HOW WOOD BURNS

Wood, man's first fuel, is actually stored solar energy. A tree's leaves function as tiny solar collectors to harness sunlight, which the tree uses to convert water, carbon dioxide, and nutrients into organic matter—wood. An act as simple as lighting a match can release this stored solar energy.

Two things must be present for wood to continue to burn: high temperature and oxygen. In order for a fireplace or wood stove to burn wood efficiently, it must retain a high enough temperature and provide enough oxygen to burn as much of the wood and its gases as possible.

When wood burns, it goes through three phases of combustion:

**1. Moisture is evaporated from the wood by the surrounding fire.** All wood (unless it's been oven or kiln dried) contains a certain percentage of

moisture. Because part of the fire's heat is used to evaporate this moisture, it's far more efficient and also much less polluting to use seasoned wood (20 percent moisture) instead of green or freshly cut wood (50 percent or more moisture). The first phase is complete when the wood reaches 212°F/100°C (the boiling point of water).

**2. As temperatures rise, wood breaks down into volatile gases and charcoal.** The wood "catches fire" at 500°F/260°C to 600°F/315°C, burning the charcoal and a small percentage of the gases. Most of the gases, however, will escape up the flue unless the temperature inside the stove is sufficiently high to burn them (phase 3). Once in the flue,

the unburned gases will combine with vaporized moisture to form creosote inside the chimney.

**3. Volatile gases and charcoal burn.** Charcoal begins to emit heat and burn at about 1,100°F/540°C to 1,300°F/705°C, reducing itself to ash. Called the coaling process, this is when wood ordinarily produces the most usable heat.

The volatile gases will ignite when they reach a temperature of 1,100°F/600°C to 1,200°F/650°C, provided they have enough oxygen supplied at the point of combustion. The gases rarely reach this temperature unless they're restricted in some manner and rerouted over the flame of the fire or to an area where these high temperatures have been achieved. Part of a noncatalytic stove's heating efficiency depends on its ability to do this.

to all parts of a room. As with the other types, their efficiency is improved if combustion air can be ducted from outside, although this may be difficult for remodelers, especially in the case of slab floors or upper-story installations.

## GAS FIREPLACES

An increasingly popular alternative for home owners who want both space heating and the romantic feel of a fireplace, gas fireplaces look like conventional ones but have artificial, fireproof logs and hidden gas jets that ignite with a flick of a switch.

Gas fireplaces come in a variety of designs. Since there's no cutting, splitting, or hauling of wood, they're much easier to maintain than wood-burning fireplaces. Also, gas burns cleanly, so no creosote builds up in the chimney. But for some, the noiseless, odorless burn of gas does not adequately compensate for the absence of the crackling sounds and rich aroma of burning wood.

Before investing in a gas fireplace, you may want to inquire about the cost and availability of natural gas in your area. Note also that installation must be done by a professional, since it involves tying into gas lines.

## WOOD STOVES

As heaters, wood stoves are more practical and economical than fireplaces. With a plentiful wood supply and proper installation, a wood stove can pay for itself in a few years, especially in areas where utility rates are high.

But using a wood stove to heat part or all of your home is also a lifestyle decision, especially if you're used to regulating heat with a thermostat. Finding, buying, carrying, splitting, and stacking wood, as well as stocking and tending the fire and dumping the ashes, are chores you have to enjoy, because they become part of your life.

In return, they lend an esthetic charm to a room and radiate a uniquely sensuous warmth. The stove itself can be an attractive addition to your home—it may, in fact, become a member of the family.

Although stoves come in many different designs, they fall into three categories: conventional stoves, fireplace inserts, and pellet stoves. For installation help, see page 97.

## CONVENTIONAL WOOD STOVES

Conventional stoves are basically metal boxes made of cast iron or welded steel, although the outside skin may also be ceramic tile or soapstone. Inside the stove is a firebox, which is sometimes lined with refractory brick.

These stoves can be either radiant or convective (shown below).

■ *Radiant heaters* are the most common type of conventional stove. In such

## Radiant & Convective Heat-exchange Systems

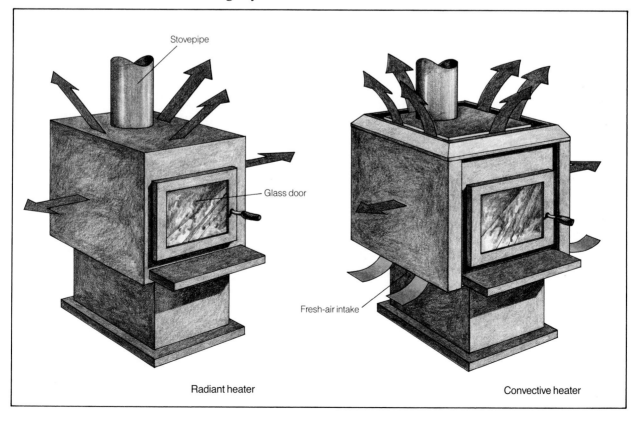

Stovepipe

Glass door

Fresh-air intake

Radiant heater

Convective heater

## Pellet Stove

*Clean and convenient, new pellet stove burns wood by-products compressed into small pellets and automatically fed into fire.*

stoves, the metal box is heated by fuel combustion, and the heat is conducted through the walls of the stove and radiated into the room.

■ *Convective, or heat-circulating, wood stoves* provide more even heat distribution than radiant types. The firebox is encased in a metal shell that's vented.

Cool room air is pulled into the stove through vents near floor level. After being heated by the firebox, the air exits through the stove's upper vents by natural convection, although some stoves, including the new pellet type (see at right), use small fans to augment the movement of the heated air.

Convective stoves also heat by radiation, but the outside surfaces don't heat up as fast as the surfaces of radiant heaters. This makes convective stoves slower to heat the room than radiant heaters, but it also makes them much less hot—and therefore safer when children are nearby. Generally, heat-circulating stoves don't need as much clearance from combustibles as radiant ones.

**Controlled combustion.** One of the key elements of a conventional wood stove is that the stove operates on the principle of controlled combustion. In a fireplace, there's no way to completely restrict the amount of air feeding the fire; thus, the fire burns uncontrolled and uses large amounts of wood. Most of the heat flies up the chimney.

In a stove, the burning rate is controlled either by adjustable air inlets on the stove itself or by thermostatic control units. This allows the home owner to control the amount of heat that's emitted into the room.

**New stove technologies.** Recent state and federal government regulations regarding air pollution have forced wood stove manufacturers to incorporate new design features into their products. The technologies developed for wood stoves have both increased heating efficiency and reduced emission levels for particulate matter and carbon monoxide.

For a closer look at how today's stoves work, see the facing page.

## FIREPLACE INSERTS

Many fireplace inserts—wood stoves that are designed to be placed in an existing fireplace—combine elements of both radiant and convective designs. They have large radiant surfaces that face the room and circulating jackets on the other sides to capture heat that would otherwise go up the chimney.

Because they utilize an existing chimney, eliminating the need to build a new one, fireplace inserts have become very popular. However, because most masonry chimneys are much too large for these stoves and do not warm up sufficiently to prevent creosote buildup, you'll probably have to install a chimney liner in order to accommodate the insert. Otherwise, you risk a dangerous chimney fire.

## PELLET STOVES

Relatively new on the market, pellet stoves are so named because they burn small pellets made from wood by-products rather than logs. Although they're the most sophisticated of all wood stoves (a microprocessor directs the operation), the basic idea for pellet stoves was borrowed from the old coal burners of the last century.

An electric auger feeds the pellets from a hopper into the fire chamber where air is blown through, creating a superheated firebox. The fire burns at such a high temperature that the smoke is literally burned up, resulting in a very clean burn, and no chimney is needed. Instead, the waste gases are vented to the outside through a duct, much the same way a clothes dryer is vented.

An outside air intake is operated by an electric motor; another small electric fan blows the heated air from the fire chamber into the room. The microprocessor controls the operation, allowing the pellet stove to be controlled by a thermostat.

Pellet stoves are easy to operate and can burn for up to 80 hours without having to be refueled. An additional advantage to such stoves is that the pellets come in easy-to-store plastic sacks, eliminating the need to cut, haul, and stack firewood.

# STOVES THAT BURN TWICE

Strict air pollution standards recently enacted by both state governments and the federal government have forced wood stove manufacturers to design stoves that burn cleaner and up to 90 percent more efficiently than ever before.

When wood burns, it breaks down chemically into charcoal and volatile gases, or smoke. In order to burn efficiently, a stove must burn both the charcoal and the smoke. But the two have different burning requirements and characteristics.

Charcoal needs to reach only about 500°F/260°C to ignite; therefore, it can be burned in the firebox. Smoke, however, must reach about 1,200°F/650°C before it burns, which would

make the wood stove too hot for the room.

This was the problem manufacturers faced in developing the two wood stove technologies now used for better burning—catalytic and noncatalytic. Both of these basic types are illustrated below.

■ *The catalytic combustor* is the first and oldest antipollution technology; it works much like the smog device on a car. All surfaces of the combustor are

coated with catalytic metals—platinum, palladium, rhodium, or a combination.

Once the unit is warmed to about 500°F/260°C, the smoke molecules, which are channeled through it, are chemically changed and ignited, thus adding heat and reducing pollutants. Catalytic combustors are typically used in wood stoves designed to heat areas over 2,000 square feet.

■ *Noncatalytic technology* is utilized in the remaining stoves. A metal baffle at the top of the firebox captures the superheated gases, and fresh oxygen is added to induce a secondary burn. Many stoves add a third and fourth burn area within the firebox. The smoke is literally burned up and the heat radiated.

## Two Wood Stove Technologies: Catalytic & Noncatalytic

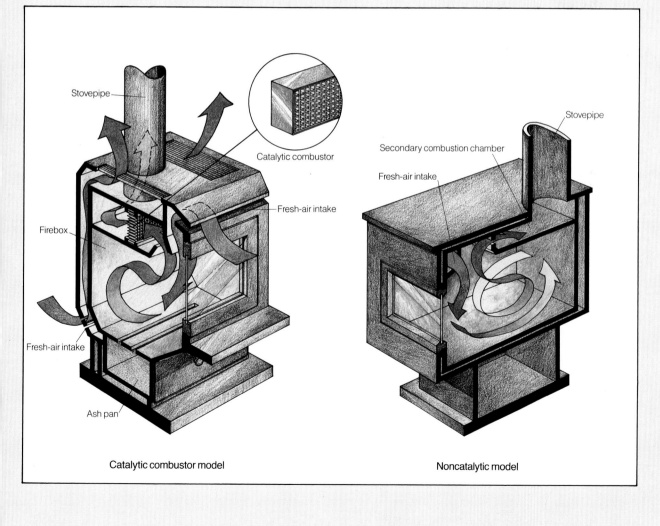

Stovepipe

Catalytic combustor

Fresh-air intake

Firebox

Fresh-air intake

Ash pan

Catalytic combustor model

Stovepipe

Secondary combustion chamber

Fresh-air intake

Noncatalytic model

# A SHOWCASE OF GLOWING IDEAS

*From the elegantly traditional fireplace to the high-tech pellet stove, the eclectic collection of fireplaces and wood stoves displayed in this gallery represents some of the best of contemporary designs. If you're thinking of adding, updating, or converting a fireplace or buying a heat-efficient wood stove, browse through the next 40 pages for attractive and adaptable ideas.*

*You'll find a variety of styles, settings, and materials. Although fireplaces were once located only in living areas and wood stoves were hidden in kitchens, they're now found throughout the house, even in bathrooms. More than just pretty faces, they often replace or supplement conventional heating systems. To help you identify the hardest-working performers, such as heat-circulating fireplaces, hybrids, and wood stove inserts, we've highlighted them with this special symbol:* 🔥

**A place of honor**

*This tidy owner-built niche has plenty of room for its handsome occupant and for a good supply of firewood. An efficient heater, the wood stove also gets high marks for its clean burn.*

**Focus your attention**

*This energy-efficient heating system combines the effectiveness of a wood stove with the ambience of a fireplace. Tempered glass doors control the cool-air intake; vents above the firebox permit the flow of heated air into the room.*

15

# TIMELESS TRADITIONS

### Paneled beauty
*The striking mantelpiece matches the room's paneling to keep the large fireplace from dominating the walls. Both the hearth and the firebox surround are marble. Architects: Arthur B. Clark & Birge M. Clark.*

### Touch of class
*Surrounded by marble and accented with Oriental figurines, a practical factory-built fireplace is transformed into an elegant work of art. Design: Okell's Fireplace of San Francisco.*

## Hearth and home

*Conversation centers around this handsome factory-built fireplace with its tile-clad raised hearth and wooden mantel. An air-circulating system and glass doors turn this fireplace into a heat source for the room. Design: Molly Agras/Courtyard Collection Palo Alto.*

### Following the flow

*Glass doors, cool-air intakes below the hearth, and vents above the firebox permit circulating air to be warmed by convection, making this fireplace not only attractive but efficient as well. Interior design: Marlene Grant and Margaret Schroeder/The Whitney Corporation.*

### Cold-weather comfort

*Clean, easy to maintain, and a space saver, this gas fireplace ignites with a flick of a switch. The marble-clad charmer, which uses ceramic logs, is a good choice for city dwellers. Design: Anthony Hail and Okell's Fireplace of San Francisco.*

### Fire and light

*The wood and marble facing of the heat-efficient fireplace in this great room turns it into a flickering centerpiece. Glass doors keep warm air from being drawn out of the room. The ample hearth has space for firewood. Architect: Rod Wolfer.*

# SCENE STEALERS

### Sheer beauty

*Pride of craftsmanship and a love of beautiful materials are embodied in this stunning fireplace design. Copper and stone were combined with an expert hand for a truly eye-catching result. Architects: Terry & Egan.*

### Wall of glass and fire

*The bold geometry of this glass wall is barely disturbed by the insertion of a factory-built metal fireplace. Black tile and red-painted flue create color accents while offering a minimum silhouette. Architects: Batter/Kay. Design: John Snyder.*

**A subtle blend**
*The simple, Oriental-style design of this fireplace was achieved with three cast-concrete slabs and an exposed aggregate finish. The hearth neatly turns the corner to become the floor of the entryway. Architect: Henrik Bull.*

# THEY CORNER BEAUTIFULLY

### Pretty and practical

*The glass door of this stylish, three-sided, factory-built fireplace tucks away behind the hood when not in use. A filtered air-exchange system heats outside air and vents it into the room through ducts on both sides of the unit.*

### Around the corner

*The stone and concrete fireplace graciously rounds the corner at an intersection of two rooms in this traditional house. An old idea, it's still adaptable today. Architects: Arthur B. Clark & Birge M. Clark.*

### Southwestern appeal

*The facing of this adobe-style corner fireplace is constructed from cement plaster over a metal lath frame. Underneath stands a factory-built unit. Mexican tile pavers on the floor eliminate the need for a hearth. Architect: Peter C. Rodi/Designbank.*

# SPACE DEFINERS

### A new design

*This old fireplace was once part of an exterior wall. Today, it marks the end of a tiled dining area and the start of a lower-level family room. Its angled corners and brass-plated chimney surround add distinctive form and metallic sheen. Architect: Kenneth Kurtzman. Design: Caryl Kurtzman.*

### Dual viewing

*This bold fireplace, with niches for wood and books, delineates the living areas of the master bedroom suite. The see-through design allows the occupants to look at the fire from both the bedroom and the sitting room. Architect: Mark Mack.*

### A sculptured look

*White-painted brick fireplace separating living and dining areas incorporates wood storage with art. A curving shelf, set into the facing, projects slightly on the back side. Architect: Batter/Kay.*

**Sportsman's lair**
*Remingtons and Russells are featured on
the mantel and raised hearth of this textured
fireplace. A trophy from the past surveys
the sporting scene. Design: Okell's Fireplace
of San Francisco.*

## The family room steps up

This corner fireplace projects like a ship's bow into the stairway between the kitchen and family room. On the kitchen-breakfast room side, the hearth sits almost at waist height, with space for wood storage beneath the firebox. On the family room side, it's raised slightly off the floor. Architect: Rushton/Chartock.

## The Cinderella touch

A humble garage is now a cheerful family room. The addition of a dramatic fireplace, with plenty of space for wood storage, gave the room its focal point. Architects: Ann Agnew and Don Boss.

# FIREPLACE FACE-LIFTS

### High-tech heating

*Replacing a factory-built radiant fireplace with this more effective hybrid increased heating capacity dramatically. Controls let you regulate the rate of burn. Design: Anchor Fireplaces.*

### Trimming down

*Once, a stone facade made this fireplace appear bulky. Now updated, it matches the room's decor. Design: Thomas Bartlett and Okell's Fireplace of San Francisco.*

## Visual links

To make a living room and kitchen seem larger, the upper half of a separating wall! was peeled away, and the kitchen counter and shelf space were extended all the way into the living area. For unity, the redesigned fireplace and hearth were faced with the same granite used on the kitchen counters. Architect: Paulett Taggart.

### The light touch

Adding its own visual statement to the room are the clean, crisp lines of this modern fireplace. Before a makeover, the fireplace was hidden behind a used brick facade. Design: Okell's Fireplace of San Francisco.

# CHIMNEY TREATMENTS

### A metallic differenc

*Copper chimney facing and mantel len
drama to a basic radiant fireplace of painte
brick. Sheets are joined with standin
seams for more design interest. The heart
becomes a built-in seat, its quarry tile con
plementing both copper and flame. Desig
W. R. Queirol*

### Almost invisible

*Easily positioned in front of a window, this
freestanding fireplace doesn't obstruct the
view. The tall, slim chimney adds even
another dimension to the house's geometric
elegance.*

## Center stage

*A massive, poured-in-place fireplace highlights the 100-square-foot living room of this well-designed cabin. Built-in seating, a high ceiling, and tall windows keep the fireplace from dominating the space. Design: Charles Barnett.*

## Plaster and prefab

*A factory-built metal firebox and its attendant stud framing combine with gypsum board and plaster to create a distinctly Mediterranean effect. The play of light and shadow and a single bright tapestry are the only decorations. Architect: Richard Ellmore Associates.*

# RAISED FOR EFFECT

### A key ingredient

*Visible over the counter, from the breakfast nook, or from the office, this tile-clad, factory-built model unifies the kitchen area and offers plenty of room below the firebox for wood storage. Design: Nan Rosenblatt.*

## Family room favorite

*Marble swirls cover the hearth and face the front of this appealing fireplace. The horizontal line of its raised hearth echoes the lines of the bookcases on each side. Tempered glass doors, mounted on the front of the firebox, help eliminate room drafts. Design: Okell's Fireplace of San Francisco.*

## Eye-level appeal

*The raised hearth extends well beyond the fireplace to form a tiled base for the open shelving at its side. Well-placed lights add an even warmer glow to the room.*

# ALL THROUGH THE HOUSE

### Welcome adjunct

*Striking in its simplicity, this clean-burning gas fireplace can be placed almost anywhere—it needs no chimney and throws off no sparks. A movable glass screen can be positioned in front of the opening, if desired. Design: Anthony Hail and Okell's Fireplace of San Francisco.*

### A comfortable retreat

*This bedroom's tidy, see-through fireplace has a lightweight factory-built core that requires no special structural reinforcement. Glass doors stop air leaks and interior drafts, increasing warmth to both bedroom and bath.*

**Under the roof**

*A steep roof and an empty attic provided the raw material for this elegant master suite. The relatively light weight of the factory-built fireplace and its ease of installation made it a good choice for the bedroom alcove.*

## Covered storage

*Display shelving divides the breakfast area from the sunken fireside family room. A tile-topped raised hearth provides extra seating; the window seat at the right covers a storage bin for firewood. Architect: Hiro Morimoto.*

### A swirl of color

*Showy marble insert and hearth dramatize this bedroom fireplace. Brass-trimmed doors control drafts handsomely. Design: Okell's Fireplace of San Francisco.*

### An affair of the hearth

*The white brick fireplace with its simple mantel unifies the eating and food preparation areas in this spacious, stylishly traditional family kitchen. The radiant-heating fireplace is used more for effect than warmth. Architect: William B. Remick.*

# THEY STAND ALONE

### A contemporary classic

*Views from the corner of the house were preserved through the use of the classic free-stander's small silhouette. Like most free-standing metal units, it's a better heater than a conventional fireplace. Architect: James A. Jennings.*

### Warmth from all sides

*Swirling air currents inside this attractive solid brass and glass fireplace ensure a long, thorough burn with minimum residue. The moving air also helps keep the glass clean.*

### Sleek styling

*The large opening in this space-saving fireplace allows maximum heating and viewing. A unique cast-iron cooking grill adds to its appeal.*

### A warm palette

*Under the colorful shell of this freestanding fireplace, a refractory brick lining encourages combustion and releases heat for hours after the fire is out.*

**Placed for display**

*Raised corner hearth gives this fireplace maximum visibility, yet keeps it out of the flow of traffic. Mirrored wall behind the fireplace reflects the awning-shaded front window.*

# A RUGGED EXTERIOR

## The big idea

*With a construction resembling gigantic building blocks, this handsome, energy-saving fireplace disguises a simple steel firebox with cast concrete. The rugged texture of the tinted concrete emphasizes its bold, sculpted form. The slot above the fireplace vents warm air. Architect: Judith Chafee.*

### Stone column

*This fireplace's massive facing hides an efficient, heat-circulating system. Cool-air intakes lie underneath the hearth; warm-air ducts vent to the sides. In addition to helping support the roof, the fireplace divides the entry and living areas, becoming, in effect, an interior wall. Architect: Don Jacobs.*

### A bold statement

*Although it resembles workmanship of a bygone era, this masonry fireplace with its well-matched stone facing is a newcomer. Paying heed to these more energy-aware times, brass-bound glass doors were added to avoid drafts.*

# CLASSIC COMBINATIONS

### Take a bow
*Perky little freestander is the center of attention in cool weather. An efficient performer, it becomes an airtight stove when the doors are closed. Controls let you adjust the rate of burn.*

### So much to enjoy
*Elegant Italian marble and a white wooden mantel complement the clean lines of this flush-mounted fireplace insert. Cool air comes in under the firebox, is heated, and flows out of the convection chamber through the top grills.*

### Attention to detail
*Painted to match the color of the rug, this hearth-mounted fireplace insert acts just like a wood stove but has a built-in look. Energy-efficient, it combines radiation and convection to heat the room.*

### Igniting the imagination
*This self-contained hybrid fireplace draws in cool air from the outside, warms it, and circulates it throughout the house. The door keeps warm air from being drawn out of the room. The raised brick hearth includes space for wood storage.*

# COZY TOUCHES

**Gilded beauty**

*Tarnish-free gold coating on the door, column, and front face is an option on this attractive pedestal stove. A large heat exchanger and a powerful fan assure maximum efficiency.*

**Simply stylish**

*Blending well with its tile hearth, this little wood stove is powerful enough to turn any master bedroom into a warm retreat. For the joy of an open fire, simply remove the glass doors and add a fire screen.*

**A big heart**

*Even heat output and easy operation are just two benefits of this well-designed stove with its large firebox. Shown here in basic black, it's also available in colors to match your decor.*

# SUPERIOR SOLUTIONS

### A fiery spirit

*A better heating source than the former radiant fireplace, the wood stove's removable doors still let the home owners enjoy an open fire.*

### Quick-change artist

*With its doors open, the double-walled stove is a fireplace; close them, and it becomes an economical heater. It was installed over decorative tiles embedded in a fire-retardant base. Architect: Rushton/Chartock.*

## Where's the chimney?

*You don't need one with the sophisticated pellet stove. The fire's high heat burns up the smoke, and waste gases are simply vented to the outside. Automatically fed with pellets, the energy-efficient stove can burn for up to 80 hours without refueling.*

## Tailored to fit

*Snug in its corner, this wood stove is a serious heater, powerful enough to warm several rooms. The stove's glass doors swing aside, to be replaced by a protective screen for fireside viewing.*

**Bask in the warmth**

*Top performance, easy operation, and low maintenance are only a few of the virtues of this well-designed stove. A ceramic-fiber blanket scrubs the smoke for clean burns, and a beveled firebox keeps the wood away from the glass for better fire-viewing.*

## An Irish import

*Although the door with its spiderweb design looks delicate, it's cast from solid iron. A large ash pan, hidden behind a separate door, slides out for easy cleanup.*

## Add some color

*A colorful contrast to its brick and tile setting, this good-looking wood stove is well designed for safety. Heat shields cover the bottom and rear of the stove; extra shields on the pipe provide additional protection.*

# SIMPLICITY OF FORM & FUNCTION

❋

### Push the button

*An electronic ignition system starts the fire roaring in this gas stove. Flames dance above ceramic logs to create the appearance of an authentic wood fire. Match the color of the easy-to-clean porcelain enamel finish to your room.*

❋

### The latest word

*This attractive pedestal stove with its large glazed door can also be used as a fireplace insert. Its wooden handle always stays cool to the touch.*

### Put the kettle on

*Accented with brass trim, this handsome hard-worker is easy to operate and provides a long, clean burn. Its high-tech combustion design gives more heat with less wood.*

### Updated concept

*The original Franklin stove, a combination fireplace and heater, was not airtight. Today's more energy-efficient model gives you the option of watching the flames without disturbing the heating action. Simply replace the fire screen with optional glass doors that unfold from the sides of the stove. Design: Okell's Fireplace of San Francisco.*

# ATTRACTIVE ADDITIONS

### Graceful demeanor

*Trim good looks make this cast-iron stove a favorite. Brick pavers form a corner hearth with plenty of space for firewood, tools, and a comfortable chair. Design: Molly Agras/ Courtyard Collection Palo Alto.*

### Vies for attention

*Even the panoramic hillside view ranks second to this high-powered wood stove in cold weather. A double-walled convection stove, it requires little space to install and usually needs no external heat shields.*

## A hard worker

*The straight lines of this high-energy wood stove blend well with the angles of the room's windows and walls. An air control in the front lets you adjust the combustion once the desired temperature is reached. Architect: Rushton/Chartock.*

## Economical replacement

*Converting this radiant fireplace to wood-stove use meant enlarging the hearth for safety. The benefits included a more economical and efficient heat source with a much cleaner burn.*

# FOR A CUSTOM LOOK

### Williamsburg inspired

*This handsomely crafted stove was patterned after an 18th-century cabinet. A curtain of fresh air washing over the inside of the door keeps smoke from building up on the glass.*

## International appeal

*A charming blue and white tile nook houses this petite French stove. Attractive to look at, it's also useful to use. A top loader, it retains heat well. Design: Molly Agras/ Courtyard Collection Palo Alto.*

## A warm glow

*Wood stove becomes the focal point of the room with the right background and hearth. Large glazed doors invite fire-watchers.*

# FIREPLACE PLANNING & DESIGN

*When fireplaces were the sole source of heat for both comfort and cooking, they were found in almost every room in a substantial house. Wherever they've been relegated to a role of supplemental heat source, it's rare to find more than one or two in a home.*

*Usually, the single fireplace is located where household members congregate to relax, converse, pursue leisure activities, and entertain guests—in the living room or family room. However, fireplaces can also lend warmth, intimacy, and beauty to bedrooms, kitchens, dens, studies, and even bathrooms.*

*Equally as important as location is the design of your fireplace. A carefully designed fireplace can warm a room not only with radiant heat but also in the way it makes the room look and feel. The most important element in how the fireplace looks is its facing—the vertical surface around the fireplace opening. The facing can be made of any of a variety of natural or synthetic materials, or a combination of them.*

*In this chapter, you'll find information on how to plan the size and location of your fireplace. Also included here are descriptions of some of the most popular facing materials and their advantages and disadvantages.*

## FIREPLACE SIZE & LOCATION

If you've been thinking about a fireplace for some time, chances are you know in some detail where you want it and how you want it to look.

Even so, asking yourself a few questions about your reasons for wanting a fireplace will help pinpoint some decisions you'll need to make regarding its size and location. Think about how often you'll have fires and with whom you'll be sharing them. Are they mainly romantic additions to an atmosphere, or will they be necessary sources of heat? The next section can help you both ask and answer these kinds of questions.

## FITTING THE FIREPLACE TO THE ROOM

Fitting a fireplace into a household means fitting it to both people and space. If the fire is to warm guests almost as often as it does the family, the hearth will need to be large enough to warm a throng, and the room big enough to hold one. At the other extreme, a hideaway fireplace will serve best if the scale is as intimate as the place.

This much is easy. But effective and functional placement calls for more than just correct size and general location. For example, putting the fireplace opening too close to a door can produce drafts that billow smoke into the room or cause unwanted traffic between the

*Rising cleanly from a raised hearth, three-sided fireplace neatly separates spacious living space. Architect: Rushton/Chartock.*

fire and those it warms. In short, you need to locate your fireplace not only in a satisfactory room, but also in a satisfactory place within that room.

The illustration below shows a number of possible fireplace locations.

**Size and shape of the room.** Both room size and shape are important in locating the fireplace and determining its size. In a small room, you'll probably be restricted to one or two wall locations. A large room offers more possibilities—and more pitfalls.

If a room is square or nearly so, a fireplace can be located with equal efficiency on any of the walls, or even in a corner. But a fireplace located on the end wall of a long, narrow room will most likely never spread its heat to the other end. Also, guests will tend to sit or stand near the fireplace, leaving the opposite end of the room empty. Arranging furniture will also be a problem. For these reasons, a fireplace in a rectangular room is generally located in or near the center of one long wall.

A fireplace wall or partial wall can be used effectively to break one overly large room into a pair of more comfortable spaces. A typical division would turn a very large living room into a living room and dining room, or perhaps into a living room and den.

Designed for such placement is the see-through fireplace (an example is shown on the facing page). Whether custom-made or factory-built, see-through fireplaces can have glass on two, three, or even all four sides so the fire's warm blaze can be seen from a number of vantage points.

Masonry fireplaces in peninsulas or islands can be built back-to-back, with the fireplace openings facing in opposite directions. These types of fireplaces are expensive to build, however, and tend to draw poorly unless designed by a specialist. It's best to build back-to-back fireplaces with two flues leading to separate fireboxes.

Irregularly shaped rooms present special problems for any fireplace that heats primarily by radiation, because infrared rays travel only in a straight line. To heat as much of the room as possible, the fireplace must be placed for optimum radiation.

One other aspect of placement has to do with the relationship of fireplace to wall. To save space in the room, you can design the fireplace so its entire depth is outside the wall (called a flush installation). To make a maximum design effect where space is no object, the whole depth of the fireplace can be inside the wall (referred to as a full projection). Or the fireplace can partially project into

the room. (All possible situations are shown below.)

**Fireplace size.** The size of a room does much to determine the size of a fireplace in both technical and esthetic terms. A huge firebox in a tiny room could bake the occupants before it cheers them. Conversely, a tiny firebox in a large living room will warm neither body nor soul.

The chart on the facing page establishes some conventional relationships of fireplace opening to room size. (Builders of conventional masonry fireplaces must take into account that all the firebox and flue dimensions relate to the size of the opening; details of these relationships are shown on page 76.)

Facings can vary enormously in proportion to openings, giving more or less emphasis to a fireplace as the designer sees fit. Even so, there are limits. The firebox should not be a peephole in a mass of stone, nor can a huge firebox look plausible surrounded by a tiny frame, or facing. Even the room's ceiling height must be taken into consideration when planning fireplace size.

**Traffic patterns.** The flow of traffic through a room affects the choice of location. Traffic patterns are determined by doorways and—less rigidly—by furniture placement. Locate the fireplace where traffic through the room won't pass between the couch and chairs and the fireplace (see illustration on page 60).

A more subtle consideration is line-of-sight views of activity outside the fireside circle. Being able to see into other rooms can break the feeling of intimacy a fireplace should create.

**Drafts.** When you locate a fireplace opposite an outside door, gusts of wind may cause an uneven flow of air whenever the door is opened, resulting in smoke billowing into the room. To prevent such drafts, build a room divider between the fireplace and the source of the moving air.

Particularly sensitive to drafts are fireplaces with two or more open sides. With these, even the faint air currents stirred by someone walking past may cause smoke to eddy into the room. The

## A Variety of Fireplace Locations

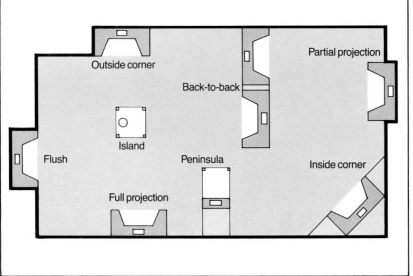

Outside corner

Partial projection

Back-to-back

Island

Flush

Peninsula

Inside corner

Full projection

most effective solution is to place furniture so that people cannot walk close by the fireplace.

**Structural limitations.** Fireplace location may be limited by the house structure itself. Installing a fireplace in a home under construction is easier and less expensive than adding one to an existing house.

If you're adding a fireplace, consider the structural changes you must make to accommodate a hearth, the firebox itself, and a chimney. A masonry fireplace, in particular, is more easily added to an exterior wall than an interior one because the foundation and chimney can be built outside. This minimizes structural alteration and loss of floor space. (For a step-by-step description of how to build a masonry fireplace, see pages 77–83.)

Factory-built fireplaces, on the other hand, require no foundation, and many have chimneys that can be fitted between studs and joists. These types of fireplaces can often be placed on an inside wall without major structural changes. (Instructions for installing a factory-built fireplace begin on page 84.) Freestanding units may be placed even more freely within existing buildings. They're installed like wood stoves (for help, see the chapter beginning on page 97).

Multiple-story buildings pose special challenges if you're adding a fireplace. For one thing, the chimney run is

*Marble-faced fireplace contributes its glow to both living room and dining room without adding bulk.*

## Good Fireplace Proportions

### SUGGESTED WIDTH OF FIREPLACE OPENINGS APPROPRIATE TO SIZE OF ROOM

| | Width of Fireplace Opening | |
|---|---|---|
| Size of Room | In Short Wall | In Long Wall |
| 10′ by 14′ | 24″ | 24″ to 32″ |
| 12′ by 16′ | 28″ to 36″ | 32″ to 36″ |
| 12′ by 20′ | 32″ to 36″ | 36″ to 40″ |
| 12′ by 24′ | 32″ to 36″ | 36″ to 48″ |
| 14′ by 28′ | 32″ to 40″ | 40″ to 48″ |
| 16′ by 30′ | 36″ to 40″ | 48″ to 60″ |
| 20′ by 36′ | 40″ to 48″ | 48″ to 72″ |

Note: Openings of factory-built fireplaces begin at 36″.

longer. In addition, if the chimney is located inside, it robs upstairs rooms of space, requires extra framing, and must avoid gas and water pipes and electrical wiring. But there is at least one advantage: if a masonry fireplace is what you want, you might look for a location that will allow you to have a hearth on the lower floor and another above it on the upper floor at a relatively low additional cost.

In some areas, local codes require that fireplaces be engineered for earthquake safety. Check with your building department for seismic considerations.

**Multiple flues.** *Never* vent more than one fireplace, stove, or other open-flame burner into a single flue. If you want to vent other burners into the fireplace chimney, each additional source of flame will require its own flue.

A chimney may contain two, three, or four flues, a situation that eliminates the need to build a separate chimney for each source of flame. Multiple-flue chimneys most often are used with back-to-back fireplaces and those located one above the other in two-story homes (see illustration on facing page). The chimney of a kitchen fireplace often includes a second flue to vent a gas or wood-burning range or barbecue grill; or you can have a barbecue grill on the outside of the unit if it can be placed on a patio or deck.

Fireplaces are often built with an extra, unused flue for future additions.

It's easier and less expensive to build an additional flue into the chimney originally than to add one later to serve a wood stove or other heat source.

**Other design factors.** Two other factors may weigh in your decision about where to locate your fireplace. One is convenient wood storage. The other is ash removal.

The need for inside wood storage will become readily apparent if you ever find yourself slogging through late night rain or snow to bring in armloads of wood. Carrying wood through the house can also leave a trail of bark chips and other wood debris. The ideal solution is a through-the-wall wood box that can be loaded from outside but used from inside. A weather-tight one minimizes heat loss from open doors.

If structural or design considerations prevent you from building such a wood box, you may want to consider designing a wood storage space alongside or beneath a raised hearth. Look through the designs pictured in the chapter beginning on page 15 for some novel wood storage ideas.

A masonry fireplace set on a foundation may be both costly and weighty, but it can offer the boon of an ash pit beneath the firebox. A factory-built fireplace cannot offer the same benefit. If you can include an ash pit, keep in mind that the most efficient kinds have two doors, one in the bottom of the firebox for dumping ashes, the other at the bottom of the foundation for removing them.

## THE FACE OF THE FIREPLACE

Although the size and design of the firebox and chimney may determine how efficient the fireplace will be, its face gives it its character and charm. A fireplace may be the centerpiece of a home; most likely, it's the focal point of the room in which it's situated. Care should be taken to ensure that the facing fits the decor both of the room and of the entire house.

You can choose from a number of different facing materials in a range of colors. You may want to design a hearth

## Controlling Traffic Around a Fireplace

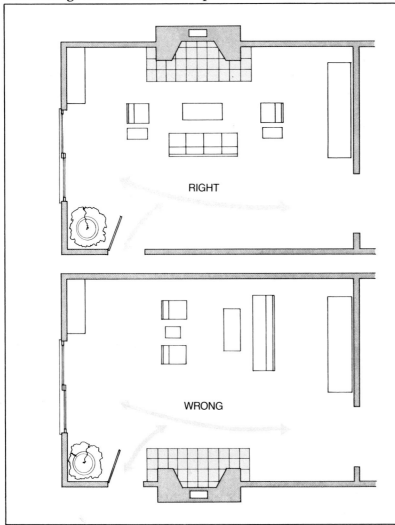

RIGHT

WRONG

## Stacking Fireplaces

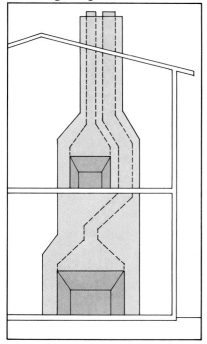

from the same material or perhaps use a different one. Just be sure that the materials complement one another.

## THE HEARTH

Sometimes referred to as the outer hearth or hearth extension, the hearth is the noncombustible material that protects the adjoining floor from sparks, runaway logs, and heat radiated from the fire. Almost all hearths are made of a masonry material.

On any fireplace set into or against a wall, the hearth must extend code-required distances beyond the front opening and to each side. The size of the hearth will depend on the size of the fireplace opening. (Details on hearth dimensions appear in the installation chapter beginning on page 73.)

Most hearths are either flush with the floor or raised above it. Space often dictates the choice: small rooms need flush hearths so traffic can move; raised hearths adapt well to large rooms to help draw attention to the fireplace. Raised hearths can be solid or cantilevered. Cantilevered types can provide under-hearth storage for wood. Both provide platforms for container plants or other decorations, and, if high enough, extra seating.

## THE FIREPLACE MANTEL

When the fireplace was used to cook the family's meals, the mantel was one of its working parts, a storage shelf for pots and pans, condiments, and bowls or dishes full of food that needed to be kept warm.

Today, the mantel, a horizontal shelf usually made of brick, wood, metal, or a synthetic masonry material, serves a decorative function. Traditional formal designs match the horizontal shelf with a vertical piece at each side of the fireplace opening. Some modern fireplace designs do away with mantels altogether, presenting a smooth, unbroken surface from fireplace opening to ceiling.

Mantels can often be ordered custom-made from mills or carvers. Manufacturers also supply them as prefabricated pieces made of wood or molded from synthetic materials.

## HOODS FOR FREESTANDING FIREPLACES

Used with freestanding fireplaces, hoods are usually made of metal, although some are masonry in a metal frame or plaster over a metal frame.

One disadvantage of hoods is that they don't draw smoke efficiently until well warmed. Because metal heats quickly, the disadvantage is less with metal hoods than with the masonry ones. (The slow draw means that many wall-mounted hoods are merely decorative disguises set above typical assemblies of firebox, smoke dome, and flue.)

## THE FIREPLACE FACING

The vertical surface around a fireplace opening is the facing. It can be of any size, up to and including the whole fireplace wall. For a colorful display of a wide range of facing materials and designs, look through the chapter that begins on page 15.

It's important to remember that the masonry materials most often used for facings are very heavy. A facing made with them may not require extra support if it's attached to a bearing wall, but it may require extra bracing or even a whole new underpinning if the fireplace fits into a nonbearing wall or is over a weak spot. The problem is most likely to arise when a heavy facing material is chosen to cover the front of a built-in fireplace, which doesn't have to be supported as strongly as a masonry fireplace.

**Brick.** The warm tones of brick blend amiably with the red orange glow of the flames and coals in your fireplace. Brick, along with stone, has long been the traditional fireplace facing.

Bricks do not have to be laid in conventional courses. They can be laid up-ended or stacked to produce a strong vertical line or be laid in massive numbers to make a wall or partition. They can also be set into the wall in the familiar patterns of the garden walk—herringbone, crisscross, or basket weave.

There are a number of different types of bricks from which to choose, including new brick (sometimes called face brick); common brick, a porous, rough type; and used brick, which has bits of mortar adhering to it and may be chipped here and there. Another variation is the long, thin Roman brick, which gives strong horizontal lines. Bricks also come in a variety of colors and hues, from red to coral to buff.

Bricks are usually available at building supply outlets (look under "Building Materials" in the Yellow Pages) and often at landscape design centers. For help with installation, consult the *Sunset* book *Basic Masonry Illustrated.*

Brick is heavy—you may need to add structural supports if it's used in mass.

**Stone.** As a fireplace facing material, stone comes in many shapes, sizes, colors, and textures.

Weathered stone offers a range of all these qualities. River rock has been rounded and polished by strong river currents; fieldstone, weathered only by climate, tends to be rough textured and angular. They're at their most effective in rustic decors, especially in their native sites. The property owner who can find stone for the taking can save a great deal of money while gaining a uniquely appropriate fireplace.

Cut stone can be almost as rugged as weathered stone if only rough-quarried, as sandstone often is, or polished to elegance, as marble and slate often are. The more work it takes to prepare the stone and the rarer the type, the more expensive it is.

Like brick, stone is heavy; when used in quantity, it may require additional support.

**Ceramic tile.** Because its colors range from earth tones to iridescent, its patterns from solid colors to hand-painted designs, and its textures from rough to glazed, ceramic tile can enhance any decor. Tile is popular as both a hearth and a facing material. You can also use it as a decorative border around the fireplace opening or apply it to the surrounding wall.

Tile is intermediate in weight and can be applied over many existing wall surfaces (see the *Sunset* book *Tile Remodeling Handbook* for detailed installation instructions). Prices vary as much as appearance, but even the lower range is relatively expensive compared to other materials.

**Concrete.** As a facing or hearth, concrete is available formed or as precast panels. While still plastic, it can be tooled, troweled, brushed, floated, or polished to provide different textures. It can also be sculpted. Onyx or marble chips can be set into it and then ground smooth and polished to make terrazzo. If these options are not enough, it can be stained or painted to allow a range of colors.

You can also buy plain or decorative concrete blocks and stack them up, like bricks or adobe.

In short, concrete is enormously versatile as well as relatively inexpensive. Like brick and stone, a concrete facing can be heavy. Take care to ensure that it has adequate support.

**Adobe.** Spanish Colonial and American southwestern styles dominate where adobe is used as a hearth and facing material. Although it comes in blocks, adobe is often used in curved forms. Not infrequently, the blocks are plastered over and painted, but tradition also allows them to be left exposed and unpainted.

Adobe blocks tend to be heavier than brick or concrete blocks, but they're less heavy than stone. Give extra support to adobe facings that cover entire walls.

**Synthetic masonry.** If a conventional masonry wall proves impractical because of its weight or for some other reason, consider using a lightweight synthetic material instead. Your choices range from thin veneers that look like brick or stone to expanded volcanic rock weighing less than a quarter as much as natural stone of similar size.

Because of their relatively light weight, synthetic materials are especially useful on second-story fireplaces. Building supply stores can help you investigate the possibilities.

**Wood.** Long used for mantels, wood is becoming an increasingly popular choice for fireplace facings as well. Different types can be used to match any interior decor. Polished oak and other hardwoods add an elegant touch to formal interior designs. Rough-sawn softwoods, such as cedar or barn siding, enhance rustic decors.

Wood facings range widely in price, depending on the variety of wood and the complexity of the carving or milling involved. Otherwise, wood has only two modest practical limitations: it may require more maintenance than other materials, and it must be installed so that no wood edges are in direct line with the flames of the fireplace. The typical code requirement is that wood be set back at least 6 inches on all sides of the opening. Any wood within 12 inches of the opening can project no more than ⅛ inch for each 1 inch of clearance. Check your local code.

**Metals.** Copper, bronze, steel, iron, and especially polished brass have become popular choices for facings. Copper and brass are often used in smooth strips or sheets. They also can be embossed or have textured or patterned surfaces. Sheet steel can be

*Marble around firebox opening and carved stone on the outside blend harmoniously to frame elegant fireplace.*

*Tile insets, handsome wood mantel, and rounded contour of firebox opening lend grace and beauty to fireplace. Design: Sharon Kasser, Distinctive Interiors.*

Design help may come from an architect, a contractor who specializes in fireplaces, the dealer from whom you buy your fireplace, or some combination of these. You can hire an architect to do the design only, or to design the fireplace and then hire the contractor. Masonry contractors (look under "Contractors—Masonry" in the Yellow Pages) often have masonry samples and designs that can help you choose the style you want.

Dealers in fireplaces or fireplace materials may also have stock designs, but they're usually not able to work with you in your home as a contractor can.

When you're dealing with professionals, be sure to get referrals before signing any contracts. Reputable individuals or companies are willing to provide references or referrals to completed jobs.

If you hire a contractor to do the installation, check first with the state Contractor Licensing Board, which will tell you if the firm is licensed, bonded, and insured for worker's compensation.

brushed, polished, or, for color, anodized. Iron usually comes in the form of wrought ornaments to complement andirons and tools rather than as a surfacing material.

The advantages of metal include durability, light weight, and adaptability to the designs of many eras. Typically, metals are expensive when compared to stone and concrete.

**Combining materials.** Many striking fireplace designs combine a number of materials in one facing. Brick and wood are two traditional favorites. But many other combinations are also possible. For example, using marble, wood, and polished brass creates a warm yet elegant surround that complements any formal decor.

## WHERE TO GET HELP

You may find that in planning your fireplace, you need professional help for the design and installation.

*Raised marble hearth and facing warmly surround factory-built fireplace. Stepped mantel stylishly encloses facing.*

# WOOD STOVE PLANNING & DESIGN

*Making wood heat an effective alternative to conventional heating, or an important supplement to it, requires the ultimate in careful planning. Like any major home appliance, the wood stove and its installation can represent a sizable financial investment, so it's crucial to select the right appliance for the job and to position it for maximum heating efficiency.*

*Whether your taste runs to a handsomely crafted classic model or a high-technology pellet stove, the planning you do now will pay you dividends later on in increased heating efficiency. The first step is to decide how much of your home you plan to heat with your stove. A stove that's too large for your needs may produce too much heat, and attempts to lower its heat output by burning it at a low temperature can cause creosote buildup and a decrease in performance. A stove that's too small, on the other hand, may leave you shivering.*

*Another important consideration is the location of the stove within the house. If the location is chosen carefully, the stove's heat can be fully utilized. In the wrong location, the stove will heat only one area, leaving the rest of the house cold.*

*Once you've decided on a location, you'll need to choose the wood stove that's right for your situation. There are a number of different types of stoves available. If you shop carefully, you should be able to find one that meets your heating needs, enhances your home's decor, and is easy to use and maintain.*

## DEFINING YOUR NEEDS

Your wood stove can be the sole source of heat for your house or simply a supplemental heat source for a hard-to-heat room. Unless you've had prior experience with wood stoves, you may want to start with one stove to supplement your present heating system. This way you can find out if wood-burning is generally compatible with your life style.

## AREA TO BE HEATED

To help you determine the size of wood stove to buy, you first need to ask how much living space you want to heat. If you plan to take a big load off your present heating system, the best location for the stove is in the main living area. The living room, or perhaps the family room, is usually the largest room in the house; it's often centrally located, making it easier to transfer heat to surrounding rooms.

If the living space you want to heat is spread out, separated by walls or intervening rooms, you'll need a way to duct the heat to those rooms.

Once you've decided which rooms you'll be heating, you'll need to provide the stove dealer with the information outlined on the following pages.

*Nestled into a custom-built brick surround, wood stove features a built-in chimney sweep, operated by a switch on side of stovepipe section.*

**A basic floor plan.** If you're going to be heating more than one room, make a rough floor plan of the living space to be heated, indicating sizes of rooms and locations of openings (doors and windows), dividers, and partitions. (If you have the original architectural plans for your home, all this information will be readily available to you.) If you own a two-story home and plan to heat upstairs rooms, include an elevation drawing indicating rooms and the location of the stairwell.

Be sure to include the pitch and overall height of the roof to determine the amount of flue pipe required.

**Cubic feet of space to be heated.** To find the cubic feet of each room to be heated, first find the square feet of floor space (length of the room times its width) and then multiply this figure by the ceiling height. If the room is irregularly

## Locating the Stove for Maximum Radiation

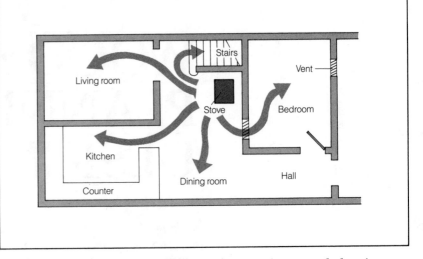

*To heat a maximum amount of living space, place stove in as central a location as possible.*

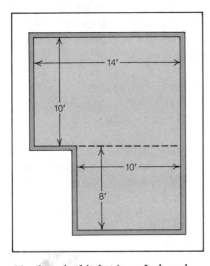

*Number of cubic feet in an L-shaped room: $(10' \times 8') + (10' \times 14') = 220$ square feet. Multiply by ceiling height $(8')$ to get 1,760 cubic feet.*

shaped, divide the area into squares or rectangles, find the square feet of each, and then add them together to get the total, as shown above.

**Heat loss factors.** If you don't already know, find out if the walls and ceilings of your home are insulated. In houses with unfinished attics, the ceiling insulation will be between the joists of the

attic floor. Note the type of insulation and its R-rating (usually printed on blanket-type insulation). If you can't find the R-rating, measure the thickness of the insulation.

To check for insulation in exterior walls and ceilings where joists are not visible from the attic, turn off the power and remove a switch or receptacle cover and a ceiling fixture. You should then be able to see if there's insulation between the wall studs and ceiling joists.

Also note the number and size of windows and whether or not windows and doors are weatherstripped. If you don't have insulation or weatherstripping and you're serious about reducing heating costs, plan to add these before you install your stove. A well-insulated house requires less heat and, consequently, a smaller stove. For more information, refer to the *Sunset* book *Do-It-Yourself Insulation & Weatherstripping*.

## LOCATING THE STOVE

Once you've determined the living space you'll be heating, you'll have to decide which room should have the stove and where the stove should go in the room. This is an important decision because the stove's location will determine how well the stove heats the living space. After they're installed, the stove,

hearth, and flue system are not easily moved.

**Which room?** Ideally, the stove should be located as near the center of the house as possible so its heat will be evenly distributed throughout the main living area, as illustrated above. In most houses, this location is likely to be the family room or living room, also the area where family members spend most of their leisure time and where family activities take place.

Of course, your heating needs may not coincide with this area. You may need a small stove in a bedroom that's never quite warm enough at night, or in a detached workshop or other room not heated by your present system.

In a two-story house, placing the stove near the stairwell, as shown in the illustration at the top of the facing page, will help heat the upstairs rooms. Or you can install floor registers to heat the room directly above the one with the stove.

If you plan to install vents or registers in the wall or floor to transfer the stove's heat to other rooms, check first with your building department. Most local building departments have code requirements on the types of vents used and their locations in the house. Your building department can advise you on these requirements.

## Heating the Upstairs

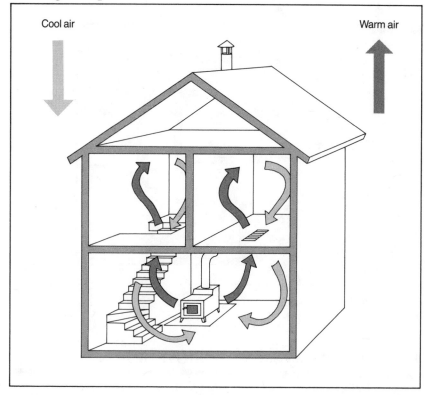

Cool air

Warm air

*Locating a wood stove near stairwell helps distribute heat upstairs. Floor vents in second-story rooms allow heat to rise naturally.*

want your stove to be, you'll have to relocate the thermostat or adjust it to compensate for the stove's heat.

**Placement within a room.** Since the stove, together with its hearth, is like a piece of furniture and will be an integral part of your room's interior design, you'll want to put it where it fits comfortably into your room decor. Also, you'll want to place the stove, like other household appliances, where it's convenient to use.

The stove's location in the room will also have an effect on its heating efficiency. If you put a radiant stove near a picture window or on an outside wall, some of its radiant heat will be lost to the outside. On the other hand, placing the stove in the center of the room will take advantage of the full radiation pattern. But since most people don't want a stove in the middle of a room, try to locate it where its heat will radiate most evenly (see illustration below).

But stove placement will be limited to where you can run the flue pipe and install the chimney. To determine this, you'll need to be aware of any obstructions imposed by the design of your

It's also a good idea to use vents that have adjustable louvers, so the vents can be closed when not in use. These vents allow you to adjust the amount of heat entering rooms—and, when closed, they also shut off noises coming from adjacent rooms.

If you have a high ceiling in your home, most of the heat from the wood stove will rise and stratify in the top few feet of the room. A good solution to this is to install a ceiling fan or two, which will cause the heat to circulate more evenly throughout the room.

On the other hand, if one room in your house is lower than the rest (such as a sunken living room), that room will probably be a bit cooler than the others. A stove in this location helps compensate for the fact that hot air rises and cool air settles at the lowest part of the house. In addition to heating the cool room, the stove's heat will also circulate more efficiently to other parts of the house.

If the thermostat for your present heating system is in the room where you

## Good Stove Location in a Room

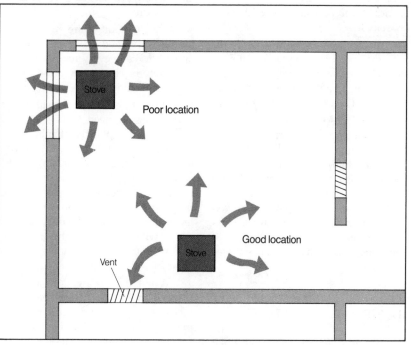

Poor location

Good location

Vent

*When a stove is located near windows, some of its radiant heat is lost to the outside. Place stove carefully for optimum radiant heat transmission.*

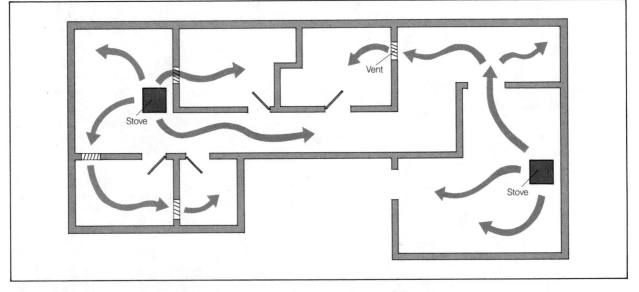

*In a home that's very spread out, you may need more than one stove to heat outlying rooms, or at least a method of transferring one stove's heat to all rooms.*

house. For help in locating the chimney connection and chimney, turn to page 101.

When deciding where your stove will go, you'll also have to take into account required clearances from combustible surfaces and materials, such as walls, furniture, and flooring. (Clearance requirements are discussed beginning on page 99.) Also consider the type of hearth you want and choose the best spot for it.

If your home is quite spread out, you may need two stoves, one at each end of the house, to provide the heat you require (see above). Or you'll need a method of conducting one stove's heat to all the rooms in the house.

Sometimes, stoves can be vented into existing chimneys or fireplaces to save the additional expense and bother of installing a separate chimney. Before deciding on such an installation, be sure to have your chimney inspected so you can determine if it's the right size and in good enough condition to use. If not, you may be able to reline it (see page 106).

## DESIRED TEMPERATURE

People are different, and so are their temperature requirements. Some people are perfectly comfortable in a room heated to 68°F/20°C; others put on their sweaters when the temperature drops below 70°F/21°C.

Most people are used to fossil fuel or electric heating, whereby every room in the house is heated, more or less, to a consistent temperature. Because the heat output of a stove fluctuates during the burning process, so will the room temperature.

Even if your entire home were heated with wood stoves, it would be difficult to keep every room the same temperature. The rooms farthest from the stove would always be a little cooler.

Often, those who heat with wood find there's no need to heat unused rooms, and they plan their family activities in the room with the stove. And you may even change your habits slightly, such as closing doors to rooms that are not in use and heating them only when necessary. You might want to throw a few extra blankets on the bed, because the fire will die down at night; or you can rely on your present heating system to make up the difference.

When discussing your heating needs with the stove dealer, be sure to include your temperature requirements. What's a comfortable temperature for you? How many rooms do you want heated to this temperature, and at what hours of the day?

## STOVE DESIGN

Traditional wood stoves are made of cast iron, steel, a combination of the two, or soapstone fit into a cast-iron frame. All have their advantages and disadvantages, but keep in mind that the quality of a stove isn't determined by the type of material used but by the thickness and the quality of the materials—and by the design of the stove.

Fireplace inserts, stoves that are placed within the firebox of an existing fireplace, and pellet stoves are two alternatives to traditional wood stoves. Both offer unique advantages over traditional stoves, but there are some disadvantages as well.

For a look at many of the various kinds of wood stoves and how they can be accommodated in actual room settings, turn to the chapter that begins on page 15.

## CAST-IRON STOVES

In cast-iron stoves, each part of the firebox is cast separately; the parts are then bolted together and the joints sealed with furnace cement. The edges of the castings are usually flanged so the seams overlap for a tighter fit. Cast-iron stove parts are thicker than those on most steel stoves, so cast-iron stoves are usually much heavier.

**Advantages.** Cast iron has long been the traditional material for wood stoves because of its resistance to warping at high temperatures or burning out after repeated firings. Cast-iron stoves will hold heat longer than thinner steel stoves, but it does take them longer to warm up.

Those who are familiar with cast-iron pans and griddles know that cast iron makes an excellent cooking surface—a consideration if you want a stove that allows you to grill food directly on the stovetop.

**Disadvantages.** Although the quality of the cast iron on stoves that meet the government's current standards has increased, cast iron is still susceptible to cracking, especially if poorly cast. It will crack if it's subjected to sudden or extreme changes in temperature, or if it's struck sharply with a heavy object, such as a log.

Overfiring a cast-iron stove or decreasing the firebox temperature suddenly (by throwing a frozen log in a hot fire or dousing the fire with water) will weaken or crack the stove.

When you buy a cast-iron stove, it must first be seasoned, or tempered, to prevent it from cracking. You do this by building a half-dozen or more small to moderate fires in the stove before using it at full capacity.

Because cast-iron stoves are heavy (some weigh more than 300 pounds), they're not easily moved. The weight of the stove is an important consideration if you plan to dismantle and store it during the summer months.

The furnace cement used to seal cast-iron stoves becomes brittle over a period of time and will fall out. This can cause the stove to lose its airtightness. When this happens, you'll have to dismantle it, reapply furnace cement, and then reassemble the stove.

**What to look for.** First, check the stove for airtightness. Part of a stove's combustion efficiency depends on how airtight it is. The so-called airtight stoves are not literally airtight—they cannot hold air or water under pressure. A good airtight stove, though, is sealed well enough so the air necessary for combustion enters only through the air inlets. Any minute quantities of air that may leak through doors or movable parts will not affect combustion efficiency.

When you shop, use a flashlight to check the stove's seams and joints carefully for possible air leaks. If the joints leak light, they will also leak air.

The most common culprit in a leaky stove is a poor seal or fit of the loading door. Inspect the door's gasket and check to see if the door fits snugly against the stove body.

Check all parts for cracks and look for pitted, porous, or rough surfaces, often a sign of poor castings. Generally, you need only compare an expensive cast-iron stove with a less expensive one to recognize quality casting. Finally, check for missing parts and make sure all movable parts work properly.

## STEEL STOVES

Steel stoves are made from sheet steel that varies in quality according to thickness. Steel thickness is measured by gauge number—the *smaller* the gauge number, the *thicker* the steel. (See the chart above, at right, to convert gauge numbers into inches.)

The pieces of a steel stove are cut out with a torch and welded together. Some steel stoves are built from several gauges of steel, with the thicker steel (12 gauge or thicker) used where it's necessary. Other stoves are a combination of steel and cast iron—an attempt to provide the best qualities of both materials. Many steel stoves, for example, have cast-iron doors to minimize warping around the door seal. The more expensive steel stoves are made from plate steel (3/16 inch or thicker) and are comparable to cast iron in durability.

**Advantages.** The lighter-gauge sheet steel stoves have the advantage of being easily portable. You can use them for temporary supplemental heat or for emergencies, such as power outages or fuel shortages. They also transfer heat more quickly than heavier stoves and thus can heat a room in a matter of minutes.

## SHEET STEEL THICKNESS

| Gauge/Thickness | | Gauge/Thickness | |
|---|---|---|---|
| 0 | 5/16 | 10 | 9/64 |
| 1 | 9/32 | 12 | 7/64 |
| 2 | 17/64 | 14 | 5/64 |
| 3 | 1/4 | 16 | 1/16 |
| 4 | 15/64 | 18 | 1/20 |
| 5 | 7/32 | 20 | 3/80 |
| 6 | 13/64 | 22 | 1/32 |
| 7 | 3/16 | 24 | 1/40 |
| 8 | 11/64 | 26 | 3/160 |
| 9 | 5/32 | 28 | 1/64 |

Approximate thickness of sheet steel gauge numbers in fractions of an inch

Heavier-gauge steel stoves have much the same heat-transfer characteristics as cast-iron stoves of the same thickness, and they can withstand high firebox temperatures equally well without cracking.

**Disadvantages.** Warping can be a problem, especially when the lighter-gauge stoves are overfired. A slight warp probably won't affect the performance of a steel stove, but it will affect the appearance. More serious warping may cause the doors to fit improperly or break welds, causing the stove to lose its airtightness. Some steel stoves have cylindrical or oval designs to help keep this warping to a minimum.

**What to look for.** As with cast-iron stoves, check steel stoves for airtightness. Make sure doors fit properly, no parts are missing, and everything works. Check the welds to be sure they're uniform and continuous; poor welds are pitted or uneven.

## SOAPSTONE STOVES

Although they have the traditional shape and look of cast-iron stoves, soapstone stoves do have some differences. First, of course, they're made of soapstone applied over a cast-iron frame. The soapstone, usually of subtle earth tones, lends a touch of beauty to the stove; it also gives it heating characteristics that differentiate it from a cast-iron stove.

**Advantages.** The high mass of the soapstone allows it to retain more heat than a cast-iron stove; thus, it provides heat long after the fire inside has gone out. It also provides a soft, gentle heat, much like a pellet stove. Another advantage of the soapstone stove is its fine, elegant appearance.

**Disadvantages.** A soapstone stove is very heavy, which can be a problem if you want to move it or store it over the winter. It's also slower to heat up than a cast-iron or steel stove.

Like in a cast-iron stove, the furnace cement needs to be replaced periodically. In addition, soapstone can crack like cast iron. Soapstone stoves also tend to be more expensive than cast-iron or steel stoves.

## FIREPLACE INSERTS

Fireplace inserts (see page 12) are small wood stoves designed to fit into an existing fireplace and utilize the existing chimney (although in most cases, the chimney should be relined, as explained on page 106). Inserts come in a variety of sizes; some are made to be fitted into specifically designed factory-built fireplaces.

Fireplace inserts must be installed according to the manufacturer's instructions. Improper installation will not only void the manufacturer's warranty on the insert but could also lead to a dangerous chimney fire.

**Advantages.** Fireplace inserts save interior room space, since they're placed inside an existing fireplace. They also tend to be less expensive than traditional wood stoves.

**Disadvantages.** Most inserts do not produce as much usable heat as free-standing wood stoves because their location inside a fireplace prevents them from radiating heat to all parts of the room. If a heat-ducting system is used with the insert, however, it can still yield a substantial amount of heat.

## PELLET STOVES

These stoves, described on page 12, are far more sophisticated than traditional wood stoves; they're operated with the help of a circuitry board. The pellet stoves are so-named because they burn wood pellets rather than logs.

Pellet stoves are roughly the same size as traditional stoves and come in a variety of coverings, from painted sheet metal to oak and other hardwoods. Pellet-burning fireplace inserts are also available.

**Advantages.** Since pellet stoves burn pellets, there's no wood to cut and haul through the house. The pellets come in plastic bags that are easy to carry, stack, and store. Pellet stoves can be thermostat controlled; their heat is soft and gentle. Only an inch of clearance is required on the sides, and no extra floor protection is needed.

On its lowest setting, a pellet stove will burn for up to 80 hours without having to be refueled—a welcome feature for those who don't have time to constantly feed the stove.

Pellet stoves are environmentally sound for two reasons. First, they burn far more efficiently and cleanly than traditional wood stoves and therefore emit very little wood smoke. In fact, the smoke can be vented out a wall, much like a clothes dryer is vented. Also, since the pellets are generally made of wood by-products, wood mills are encouraged to recycle.

**Disadvantages.** Pellet stoves are usually more expensive than traditional wood stoves. They also require more technical expertise to install, because the computer and sensors must be calibrated. Pellet stoves are of little use when the power goes out, since they rely on electric motors. If you buy a pellet stove, have a backup source of heat that's not dependent on electricity.

## EASE OF OPERATION

When you're shopping for a stove, such conveniences as large loading doors, insulated door handles, and ash pans may seem relatively unimportant. However, if you operate your stove on a regular basis, you'll learn to appreciate the importance of these "little" conveniences.

### LOADING WOOD

Stoves with large fireboxes naturally accept larger chunks of wood, provided

## Convenience of Loading

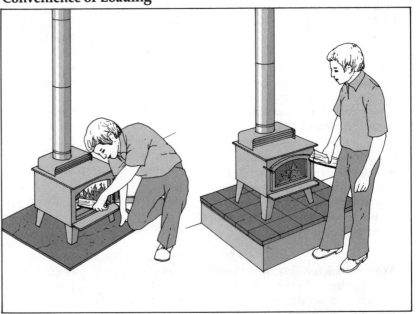

*A small stove with a low door should be placed on a raised hearth to avoid having to bend down to load it.*

the pieces fit through the loading door. A large firebox and a large loading door mean less work chopping and splitting wood. Even in small stoves, the size of the loading door should be in proportion to the firebox size.

**Location of loading doors.** The loading door on a stove can be located on the front, side, or top of the stove. Some stoves are designed with doors both in front and on top. Stoves have a tendency to puff smoke back into the room when the doors are opened too fast, or if the loading door is too large for the firebox.

On front-loading stoves, make sure the door is at a convenient height. If the door on the stove is too low, you'll have to stoop to load the wood unless you place the stove on a raised hearth (see illustration on facing page).

**Door handles.** The door handle on a stove should be easy to operate. When checking stoves, open and shut each door a few times; you should not have to force a door shut in order to make it seal tightly. Also, the door handle should be insulated or located where it won't overheat. The door handles, as well as the damper handles, should not get too hot to touch, even if the stove has been burning for several hours.

## ASH REMOVAL

Removing ashes from a stove can be a messy job, but many stoves now come with an easy-to-use ash bin below the firebox. These metal trays can be easily lifted and the ash dumped into a metal ash storage can.

If the stove doesn't have a removable ash bin, you'll have to remove the ash using a shovel and broom. Regardless of how careful you are using the shovel, some of the ash will fly into the room and settle on your furniture.

## OTHER FEATURES & CONVENIENCES

Some stoves have features that are not necessarily related to their ease of operation but, nonetheless, add much to the pleasure of having a wood stove.

## GLASS DOORS & WINDOWS

Part of the romance of fireplaces is being able to gaze into the flames. Most of today's stoves have glass doors that provide a similar view of the fire while creating none of the drafts of an open fireplace.

Keeping these windows clear of soot and ash can be a problem. Look for stoves with an air-wash design whereby cool exterior air is directed down and across the windows to keep them relatively free of soot.

## COOKING ON THE STOVE

Just about every traditional stove has at least enough room on top for a tea kettle; but some of the stoves used primarily for heating have larger cooking surfaces than others. Those that accommodate several pots and pans will allow you to prepare simple meals.

If you plan to do any cooking on your stove, look for one that's specifically designed for that purpose. It should have at least one pot hole with a removable lid, and a separate handle for removing the lid when you want to cook directly over the fire.

## FINISHES

Black is the traditional color for wood stoves because it was considered the best color for radiating heat and the easiest color to maintain. Today, however, stoves come in a variety of colors, from black to earth tones to pastels. Most stoves are covered with a high-temperature enamel finish.

For touch-ups, you can buy stove polish and spray cans of high-temperature enamel in most hardware stores or from your stove dealer.

## SHOPPING FOR A STOVE

Even the most durable stove will not last indefinitely, so it's important that both stove manufacturer and dealer stand behind their product. You should be assured that you're getting everything you've paid for and, even more important, that if you encounter any

difficulties with the stove later, they can be easily corrected.

## EPA GUIDELINES

All new stoves sold today come with an Environmental Protection Agency sticker (shown on page 72) that indicates the heat output of the stove in Btu's per hour. (One Btu, or British thermal unit, is the amount of heat required to raise the temperature of a pound of water by 1°F.)

The sticker provides two numbers. The smaller number is the average amount of Btu's the stove emits at low damper; the higher number is the average amount of Btu's produced at a high burn. In general, the lower the smaller number, the longer the stove will burn without refueling. Use these numbers as a guideline only; your dealer should be able to answer specific questions about heating capacity.

## STOVE DEALERS

The stove dealer you choose should have a proven track record. The dealer should be able to help you determine your needs, answer your questions honestly, and be willing to visit your home to get a firsthand look at your situation. It's preferable to work with a dealer who's an established member of your community and familiar with your area. A good dealer will be able to provide you with names of satisfied customers and the assurance that you'll be able to obtain both replacement parts and repair service should you need them in the future.

Some dealers employ their own installers. They'll be able to quote you a complete price that includes the cost of the stove as well as installation of the stove, chimney, and hearth. Others can recommend a reliable installer or will help you do your own installation.

## AVAILABILITY OF PARTS

A well-built stove should last many years before you need to replace any parts. Occasionally, however, a part may break or wear out before its time. If this happens, the part should be readily available from the stove dealer or manufacturer. Grates, steel liners, and gaskets, on the other hand, must be replaced periodically, so you want to be sure you can buy the parts you need.

The first question to ask is how long the stove manufacturer has been in business. A stove company that has been in operation for the past 10 years will probably still be around 10 or 20 years from now—and that in itself offers some assurance that replacement parts will be available.

A few cast-iron stoves have plates that are machined and fitted by hand, so they're not interchangeable. Should such a stove become damaged, you'll have to ship the whole thing back to the factory for repair and probably pay shipping costs—unless you can repair it yourself or have it done locally. On most stoves, though, the parts are interchangeable, and many stove dealers stock spare parts for their stoves.

**Guarantees.** Many stove manufacturers guarantee their stoves to indicate their durability and overall quality. Read the stove guarantee or warranty carefully. For how long is the stove guaranteed? Which parts are covered under the warranty? Is the guarantee unconditional or does it just cover defects in parts or labor?

## WHAT ABOUT COSTS?

The price your dealer quotes you for the stove should be complete. It should include any shipping and delivery costs and any stove accessories that are essential to its operation.

**Chimney and hearth materials.** The cost of chimney and hearth materials depends on the type of installation required and is figured separately from the price of the stove. Most dealers carry

flue pipe and other chimney components, and will advise you on what you'll need if you plan to install the stove yourself. Otherwise, the price of materials is usually included in the installation costs.

**Insurance.** Before you actually buy your stove, check with your insurance company. Most companies require notification of any major changes to your home that affect safety.

If you already have fire insurance, you probably won't need any additional insurance when you install a wood stove. However, the insurance company will most likely require that the stove and its installation meet certain fire safety requirements in order for your present policy to cover any fire damage caused by the installation. Some companies may refuse to pay for damage from a fire caused by unsafe installation.

## How to Read a Wood Stove EPA Label

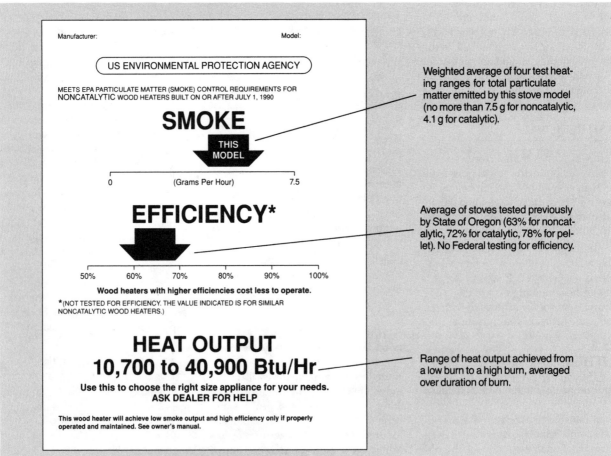

# FIREPLACE INSTALLATION, MAINTENANCE & USE

*Whether your fireplace design calls for a masonry unit with a tile facing, a sleek, freestanding model, or some other design, it's important to understand the installation procedures. Knowing the steps involved and the construction techniques required may affect the location of your fireplace, its size, and the materials you use.*

*Most masonry fireplaces are constructed by professionals, who have the technical skill and know-how to build a safe, sound structure. The same is true of factory-built units, whether installed inside or outside a wall. A freestanding unit, on the other hand, can be installed by a home owner who possesses some basic carpentry skills; however, the manufacturer's instructions must be followed to the letter to ensure safe installation and operation.*

*On the following pages, installation procedures are described for masonry, factory-built, and freestanding fireplaces. These descriptions are not meant to be exhaustive—use them only as a guide.*

*Even the best constructed fireplace can be a hazard if it's not maintained correctly. A buildup of creosote in the chimney can cause a dangerous chimney fire. Care must also be taken when laying the fire. Guidelines for safe use and maintenance appear at the end of the chapter.*

# INSTALLING A MASONRY FIREPLACE

A good masonry fireplace is not only a work of art but also a work of many skills. In order for a fireplace to operate properly, it must be built by someone with considerable expertise in masonry who follows the established rules and practices of sound fireplace construction. Even the simplest brick fireplace requires many hours of painstaking work.

Because of the time and skill involved, most home owners choose to have a mason do the work, or at least a major portion of it. Whether you're skilled enough to do the work yourself or you're hiring a professional, you'll want to understand the basic procedure.

For help with construction, consult the *Sunset* book *Basic Masonry Illustrated*.

## BASIC COMPONENTS

The components discussed below have been compiled from standard craft practices and national building codes. Note, however, that local codes and requirements may vary. Always check with your local building department before beginning any construction project. (For a look at basic fireplace anatomy, turn to page 7.)

**Foundation.** Because of its considerable weight, a masonry fireplace requires an additional foundation consisting of a footing (a reinforced concrete slab) and walls built up to hearth level.

Foundation walls may be constructed of reinforced Portland or refractory cement concrete, solid masonry, or hollow masonry blocks filled in with mortar. Walls must be at least 8 inches thick. In houses built on slabs, the fireplace is often built directly on the footing.

For details on reinforcing and pouring a concrete foundation, see Step 2 on page 77.

**Mortar.** Two separate mortar mixes are required in fireplace construction. A special refractory mortar made from fireclay mixed with water must be used in the firebox and for the fireclay flue tiles or fireclay brick. Type S mortar (1 part Portland cement, ½ part hydrated lime, 4½ parts mortar sand) is one of several mixes recommended for use elsewhere.

**Ash pit.** The ash pit should be protected from water seepage, because if the ash load becomes wet, a disagreeable, ashy odor will permeate the house.

The opening in the firebox floor is covered with a hinged or pivoting cast-iron plate to allow ashes to drop into the pit below. Select a type that cannot drop accidentally into the pit when opened.

For easy ash removal, locate the sill of the cleanout door about 10 inches above grade and cover the bottom of the pit with mortar sloped toward the door.

For a second-story fireplace directly above a first-story one, the ash chute must be routed around the fireplace below. To avoid clogging, the slope of the chute should not be greater than 6° from vertical.

**Facing.** For safety, the nearest edge of combustible trim, paneling, or facing should be set back at least 6 inches from all sides of the fireplace opening (see the information on wood facings on page 62). Since local codes may vary, check with your building department. Maintain a minimum clearance of 2 inches between all wood framing members and the fireplace or chimney masonry. The outer hearth should be at least 8 inches wider on each side than the fireplace opening and should extend into the room a minimum of 16 inches from the edge of the opening. Larger hearths are required for fireplaces with openings greater than 6 square feet.

**Firebox.** The inner hearth and the reflecting walls should be made from 4-inch-thick firebrick bonded with fireclay mortar. Bricks are laid flat and held in place by metal ties bonded into the main masonry walls.

If you build the back wall in an upward curve that slopes into the fireplace, both smoke and rising currents of warm air will flow into the room. To avoid this, the back wall should rise in straight planes to the level of the edge of the throat. For building details, see Steps 11 and 12 on page 80. Optimum firebox dimensions are given in the chart on page 76.

**Lintel.** The minimum lintel required to support the masonry above the front of a moderately wide fireplace opening is an angle iron 3½ by 3½ by ¼ inches that's long enough to give a 3- or 4-inch seat on the masonry. For heavy masonry and wide openings, the sizes and thicknesses of these steel lintels increase in proportion. To provide for expansion, wrap the ends with fiberglass wool or provide some means for the steel lintel to move when heated.

You can build a masonry arch successfully if, at the sides of the opening, the masonry is sufficiently reinforced to resist the thrust of the arch. The masonry arch should be at least 4 inches thick, preferably more to avoid sagging.

**Damper.** Many types of dampers are available; most are combined with a metal throat. Some operate with a push-pull handle, some with a poker, and others with a twist handle. A manufactured smoke dome contains a damper with "open" and "close" chain controls that hold the damper in the desired position. Any type of damper installed according to the manufacturer's instructions should be satisfactory. Set the damper loosely in place and wrap the ends in fiberglass wool to allow for expansion.

**Throat.** The throat, or damper opening, should extend the full width of the fireplace opening and have an area not less than that of the flue. Up to the throat, the sides of the fireplace should be vertical; about 5 inches above the throat, the sides should start drawing into the flue. The bottom edge of the throat should be at least 6 inches above the bottom of the lintel.

The throat can be made of masonry. To save time and labor, you can install a metal prefabricated throat or smoke dome.

**Smoke shelf.** The smoke shelf should run the full width of the throat and be at least 6 inches front to back (size depends on the depth of the fireplace). It should have a smooth, concave surface.

**Smoke dome.** The smoke dome extends between the side walls from the top of the throat to the bottom of the flue. Slope the side walls at a 60° angle from horizontal and smoothly plaster them with cement mortar or an equally smooth interior surface so as not to diminish the draft action.

**Flues.** Flues are lined with fireclay flue tiles or fireclay brick to protect the surrounding brickwork in the chimney from the effects of hot flue gases. Tiles or bricks should be set with fireclay mortar, and joints should be smooth to assure proper draft and to reduce creosote buildup.

Round flues are considered the most efficient for draft and smoke removal because draft-smoke columns ascend in spirals. Corners of square or rectangular flues are ineffective areas, contributing little to the proper working of a flue. Square or oblong flues are often used, however, because they're easier to set in place.

**Multiple flues.** If you plan to locate two or more flues in the same chimney structure, they must be separated by at least 4 inches of a masonry material such as brick, mortar, or concrete. This masonry divider, called a wythe, should extend 6 inches or so above the chimney top to prevent smoke from one flue from being drawn down the other. Another way to avoid this problem is to make one flue slightly taller than the other.

The size of the flue will be dictated by the size of the fireplace. The chart on page 76 gives the recommended flue sizes for sea level installations (see "Chimney height," above, at right, for information on the effect of altitude).

Flues have better draft if they're built as close to vertical as possible. When a change in direction is necessary, it should not exceed 30° from vertical, nor should it reduce the flue area at the offset angle.

**Chimney materials.** A variety of masonry materials, including brick, concrete blocks, clay tiles, poured concrete, and stone, may be used in constructing chimney walls. Following are the recommended thicknesses for walls of these materials. These thicknesses do not include the thickness of the fireclay flue liner. Tall chimneys, or ones exposed to high winds, may require thicker walls. Check with your local building inspector.

*Brick:* Not less than 4 inches thick; for exterior chimney walls exposed to severe weather, not less than 8 inches thick, or two courses laid flat.

*Hollow concrete blocks (filled with mortar):* Not less than 6 inches thick.

*Poured concrete or solid concrete blocks:* Not less than 4 inches thick; exposure to severe weather conditions may warrant additional thickness. Poured concrete chimneys require both vertical and horizontal lacing of steel reinforcing bars.

*Stone:* Not less than 12 inches thick.

**Chimney height.** In order to draw properly, the chimney must extend at least 3 feet above the roof opening (measured from the uphill side on sloped roofs) and at least 2 feet above the roof's highest point within 10 feet of the chimney. For more information on how to measure for a chimney, turn to page 86.

At elevations above 2,000 feet, both the height of the chimney and the cross-sectional area of the flue should be increased by 5 percent for every 1,000 feet of elevation. Consult your local building department for detailed figures.

**Chimney clearances.** An air space must be left between all wood framing members and the outside surface of chimney walls. Clearances may vary, depending on the structural members (studs, beams, joists, or girders) and local code requirements, although a 2-inch space is considered standard in most codes. Spaces between the chimney and framing are firestopped with metal flashing or strips of metal lath covered with plaster.

**Seismic reinforcement.** If you live in an area subject to earthquakes, the chimney must be strengthened with vertical reinforcing bars extending the full height of the chimney. Local codes will determine their size, number, and placement. In addition, the chimney must be anchored at each floor or ceiling line unless built completely within exterior walls. For details on anchoring, see Step 18 on page 82.

**Chimney caps.** Such caps, often referred to as termination caps, prevent snow and rain, animals, leaves, and other unwanted objects from falling down the chimney and clogging the flue, coming to rest on the smoke shelf, or entering the house. They also separate the flue from the air-cooled chimney passages and minimize exterior wind disturbances.

Chimney caps that are equipped with integral spark arresters can prevent sparks from drifting out of the chimney and starting a serious fire. Having such a cap is especially important if you have a wood shingle or shake roof or you live in an area with numerous tall trees. In many localities, building codes require that chimneys be fitted with this kind of chimney cap. Be sure to consult your local building department to see if they have this requirement.

Use rust-resistant wire mesh or perforated sheet metal with openings no smaller than ½ inch and no larger than ⅝ inch. The top of the screen should be at least 12 inches above the cap.

## TYPICAL FIREPLACE DIMENSIONS

| Opening width | Opening height | Firebox depth | Back wall width | Vertical back wall height | Inclined back wall height | Rectangular flue lining | Inside diameter of standard round flue lining |
|---|---|---|---|---|---|---|---|
| 24″ | 24″ | 16″–18″ | 14″ | 14″ | 16″ | 8½″ by 8½″ | 10″ |
| 28″ | 24″ | 16″–18″ | 14″ | 14″ | 16″ | 8½″ by 8½″ | 10″ |
| 30″ | 28″ | 16″–18″ | 16″ | 14″ | 20″ | 8½″ by 13″ | 10″ |
| 36″ | 28″ | 16″–18″ | 22″ | 14″ | 20″ | 8½″ by 13″ | 12″ |
| 42″ | 28″ | 16″–18″ | 28″ | 14″ | 20″ | 8½″ by 18″ | 12″ |
| 36″ | 32″ | 18″–20″ | 20″ | 14″ | 24″ | 8½″ by 18″ | 12″ |
| 42″ | 32″ | 18″–20″ | 26″ | 14″ | 24″ | 13″ by 13″ | 12″ |
| 48″ | 32″ | 18″–20″ | 32″ | 14″ | 24″ | 13″ by 13″ | 15″ |
| 42″ | 36″ | 18″–20″ | 26″ | 14″ | 28″ | 13″ by 13″ | 15″ |
| 48″ | 36″ | 18″–20″ | 32″ | 14″ | 28″ | 13″ by 18″ | 15″ |
| 54″ | 36″ | 18″–20″ | 38″ | 14″ | 28″ | 13″ by 18″ | 15″ |
| 60″ | 36″ | 18″–20″ | 44″ | 14″ | 28″ | 13″ by 18″ | 15″ |
| 42″ | 40″ | 20″–22″ | 24″ | 17″ | 29″ | 13″ by 13″ | 15″ |
| 48″ | 40″ | 20″–22″ | 30″ | 17″ | 29″ | 13″ by 18″ | 15″ |
| 54″ | 40″ | 20″–22″ | 36″ | 17″ | 29″ | 13″ by 18″ | 15″ |
| 60″ | 40″ | 20″–22″ | 42″ | 17″ | 29″ | 18″ by 18″ | 18″ |
| 66″ | 40″ | 20″–22″ | 48″ | 17″ | 29″ | 18″ by 18″ | 18″ |
| 72″ | 40″ | 22″–28″ | 51″ | 17″ | 29″ | 18″ by 18″ | 18″ |

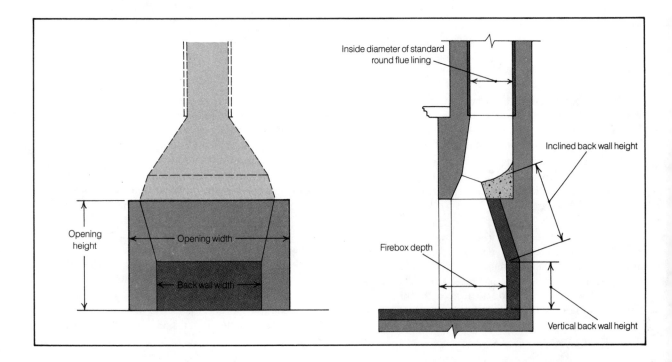

# ADDING A MASONRY FIREPLACE

The following sequence of steps shows, in a general way, the addition of a simple masonry fireplace in an outside wall. Details may differ from local building codes and practices; if so, follow local guidelines. To install a metal insert in place of a masonry firebox, smoke dome, and damper, see page 83.

**Step 1. Laying out the job.** Once the fireplace site has been located, mark lines on the outside wall to indicate the opening to be cut. Avoid locating vertical lines directly over wall studs. To locate studs from the outside, use a stud sensor, tap the wall with a hammer (the stud responds with a solid thud), or measure from a nearby door or window (studs are usually set 16 or 24 inches on center).

Boundaries of the foundation pit are staked out as shown at right. The foundation must extend at least 6 inches beyond the base of the fireplace structure on all sides.

**Step 2. Digging the foundation pit.** Dig the foundation pit about 6 inches or so beyond the boundary lines to make room for building concrete forms. The proper depth will depend on frost-line depth, soil stability, and your local building code. The sides of the pit should be as vertical as possible and the bottom smooth and level.

Build wood forms to hold wet concrete to the exact outside dimensions of the foundation slab. Place a grid of ½-inch reinforcing bars, 12 inches on center, 5 inches above the bottom of the pit. Support the grid on bricks or scrap blocks, pulling them out as you pour concrete. For added strength, bend four steel rods vertically at a 90° angle near the bottom and set them so they'll extend up into the inside corners of the rough brick firebox. (In earthquake areas, the rods must extend the full height of the chimney.) For additional reinforcement, lay rods horizontally every 2 feet around the outside wall.

Let the concrete cure, keeping it moist by covering it with damp burlap sacking or polyethylene sheets until fully cured (a week to 10 days).

**Step 3. Opening the walls.** The next step is to remove the outside wall siding and sheathing to expose the wall and floor framing. Tools and techniques used for this job will depend on the type of material covering the wall. To remove stucco, you'll need a wide mason's chisel and hammer, wire cutters, and a nail puller. Wood siding and sheathing may be cut with a hand saw, portable circular saw, or saber saw—or a combination of these.

Remove the siding down to the foundation level. *Do not remove the studs*—just clear out everything around them, including cross bracing. Any plumbing or electrical lines will have to be rerouted away from the opening.

Next, remove the inside wall covering to the dimensions of the opening. Use a tarp or thick plastic sheeting to cover the opening while it's exposed.

**Step 1**

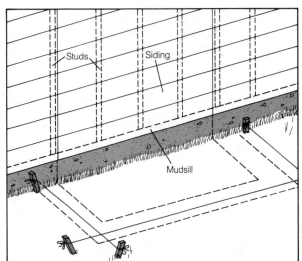

**Step 2**

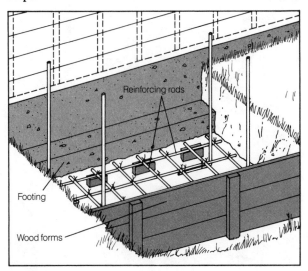

**Step 3**

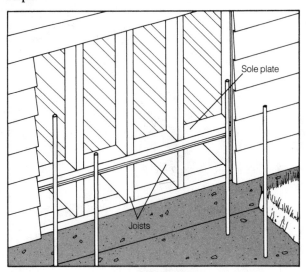

**Step 4**

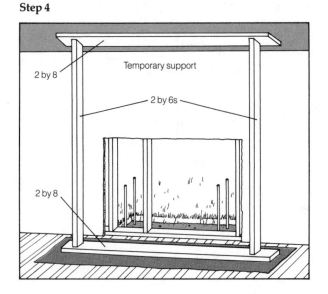

2 by 8

Temporary support

2 by 6s

2 by 8

**Step 5**

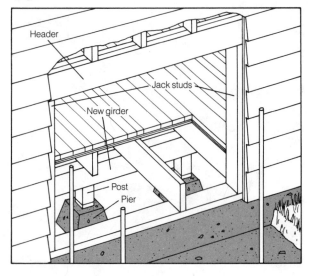

Header

Jack studs

New girder

Post

Pier

**Step 6**

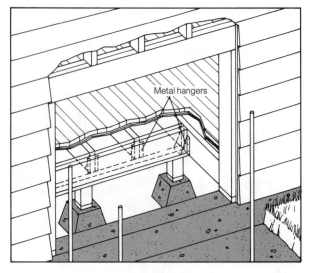

Metal hangers

**Step 4. Cutting the studs.** Don't forget that the studs are holding up your roof, as well as keeping the wall in place. Before you cut them, you'll need to make provision for carrying the load while the wall is open and temporarily weakened.

One way is to transfer the load to a temporary frame made of 2 by 6 uprights and 2 by 8 horizontals. Cut the 2 by 6s about ¼ inch longer than the measured space and wedge them between the 2 by 8s. (You may want to pad the top 2 by 8 to avoid scarring the ceiling.) Be sure to place the frame so it bears weight. If ceiling joists run at right angles to the fireplace wall, there's no problem. If they run parallel to that wall, center the support under the joist nearest the wall, not between two joists.

Once the support is in place, cut the studs flush with the top of your opening; then install a doubled header of 2 by 6s spaced so that the faces are flush with the edges of the adjacent studs, as shown in Step 5. Toenail the trimmed studs to the header. Jack studs are installed to support the header after the floor is opened.

**Step 5. Opening the floor.** The floor must be removed to the width and depth of the outer hearth. As when removing studs, you'll need support for trimmed floor joists, but in this case it will be permanent. Set a 6 by 6 girder under the joists before they're cut, placing it back far enough to allow for the later addition of a doubled header. Support the girder on precast concrete piers and posts. Depending on how much work space you have, you may do this before or after cutting away the flooring.

Once the girder is in place and the flooring is removed, trim the floor joists and cut away the sole plate but not the mudsill. Next, install a jack stud at each side to transfer weight from the header to the mudsill. Save all materials cut away; you may need them to reframe the floor opening. The temporary ceiling support can now be removed.

(If you want to avoid cutting the floor, plan for a canti-levered elevated hearth. Check with your architect and building inspector for details.)

**Step 6. Finishing the floor opening.** Finish off the floor construction by rebuilding the floor substructure so it can carry the load once borne by the joists you have cut.

First, measure and cut two lengths of 2 by 6 to fit as headers across the exposed ends of the cut joists; butt them snugly against the uncut joists on both sides of the opening and nail them firmly in place. End nail the cut joists to the header, or, as an optional step, support the ends of the cut joists in metal hangers as shown.

If uncut joists on either side of the opening are offset from the opening, use pieces cut from joists to support the floor flush with the sides of the opening. Once the floor opening is framed in, remove the section of sill across the bottom of the wall opening, exposing the foundation.

**Step 7. Building the ash pit.** Now comes the start of the brickwork. Clean all dirt off the top of the concrete foundation slab so the mortar will stick to the slab. Lay a wall two bricks wide across the front and back, one brick wide on the sides. Butt the front wall against the house foundation, making sure the brickwork maintains the required minimum clearance from wood framing and siding.

The two short walls, inside the box, do not have to be locked into the structure. They support the firebox brickwork. The vertical reinforcing rods should be embedded in masonry to protect them from rusting out. Lay bricks diagonally across the corners and fill in with mortar. In most areas, rods need extend only a short distance above hearth level, but in earthquake-prone regions, local codes usually require vertical reinforcing to reach the full height of the chimney.

Be sure to mortar the cleanout door securely in place so embers cannot escape.

**Step 8. Forming the subhearth.** With the pit finished, it's time to start the subhearth. Keep an eye on dimensions to be sure that the surface of the finished hearth comes out flush with the finish flooring. (Figure down from the floor surface.) Allow for the thickness of the finished hearth material, a bed of mortar (at least ½ inch thick), and at least 6 inches of concrete subhearth under the firebox.

Wooden forms hold the outer hearth in place while the concrete is setting, but wood should not be used on the inner hearth because it must be removed to conform to code, a nearly impossible task once the subhearth is in place. For the inner hearth form, use loose bricks resting on ½-inch steel reinforcing rods as shown in the drawing, or use solid brickwork or steel plates. (Some local codes may require that wooden forms be removed from an outer hearth as well. In this case, be sure you have room to work, or use a metal form.) Remember to provide for an ash dump (shown below).

Once the forms are set, place a grid of steel reinforcing rods 3 inches below the top of the slab and pour the concrete. Use a float to level the surface.

**Step 9. Finishing the subhearth.** The cut-away drawing shows the finished concrete slab in place. The slab, cantilevered out from the front wall of the ash pit, will be anchored under the weight of brickwork to be laid on the inner hearth.

Any irregularities in the concrete surface should be corrected with mortar when the finished hearth is being laid. (Failure to do so will lead to an uneven firebox floor—not critical, but unsightly and potentially hard to clean.)

Note the placement of the reinforcing steel mat. Vertical steel reinforcing rods are continued through the slab to be cemented in brickwork around the firebox.

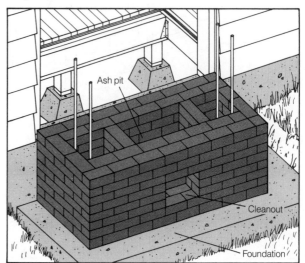

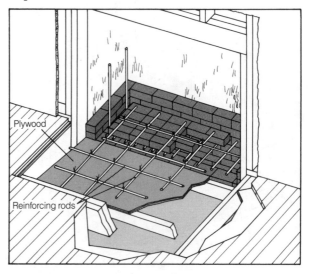

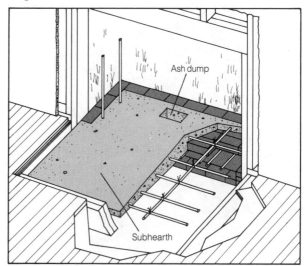

**Step 10**

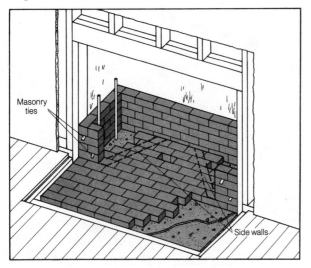

Masonry ties

Side walls

**Step 11**

Side walls

**Step 12**

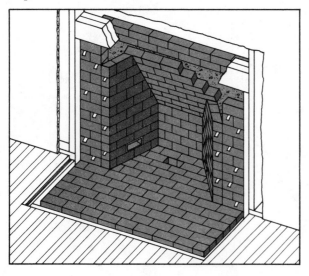

**Step 10. Finishing the hearth.** Lay the inner hearth as soon as the subhearth has had about 12 hours to set and the outer brickwork has been brought up enough courses to reach slightly above finished hearth level. The inner hearth is laid with firebrick, bonded to the subhearth with a ½-inch-thick bed of fireclay mortar.

Note that the firebrick floor covers only the area needed for the firebox. When these bricks have been laid, they're usually covered with a layer of sand to protect them from mortar drops as the masonry is built up. The outer hearth—usually laid with tile or common brick—can be set at this time or postponed until the facing is installed. Masonry ties, inserted in the mortar joints, will anchor the facing when it's attached later.

The dotted lines indicate the location of firebox side walls, which always angle inward to improve heat radiation.

**Step 11. Laying the firebox.** The firebrick walls of the firebox may be laid at the same time as the outer brickwork, or they may be held off until the outer work reaches damper height. Firebricks are laid in fireclay mortar that's been mixed to the consistency of soft butter and applied in a layer ⅛ to ¼ inch thick. Bricks are laid flat to give greater strength to the wall.

Back and side walls are laid simultaneously, one course at a time. (This must be done because the joints are a complicated set of angles; see Step 12.) An outside air intake takes the place of one of the bricks in the side wall's second course. (The vent is required if the fireplace has glass doors.) The space between the angled side walls and the outer brickwork can be filled with mortar.

**Step 12. Setting in the back wall.** Lay the back wall plumb for about 12 inches; then slope it forward to reflect heat outward and to provide for a smoke shelf. The angle of slope of this rear wall will be established by the size and height of the fireplace. The slope should form a plane, not a curve. (If the wall is curved, rising currents of warm air will not only flow into the room but will also bring smoke with them.) The rear wall should reach above the level of the lintel, to serve as the back edge of the throat and also as the back bearing surface for the damper.

Since side walls are usually laid to butt against the sloping wall, they have to be beveled at the back end to meet the angle of the wall. One way to cut side walls is to put each course of brick in place dry, hold a straight board (slanted at the proper angle) against the rear edge of the wall, and draw a line along the edge. Disassemble the upper course, cut the rear bricks on the line, and mortar the course into place.

After both side walls are laid, the sloping back wall can be mortared in. Tip the first course above the straight wall by making a wedge-shaped joint higher in back than in front.

**Step 13. Providing a damper and smoke shelf.** Except for smoke domes that both eliminate part of the masonry and have an incorporated damper, dampers fall into two main categories: blade and dome dampers. In the blade type, the damper door is hinged or swiveled in a flat frame. In the dome type (shown at right), the door is fitted into a metal housing shaped into a throat. Some dome dampers, such as the one shown here, are designed with a front edge that serves as a lintel for the fireplace facing, but most of them simply support the masonry of the inner brickwork. In the latter case, a lintel is installed to support the facing after the damper is in position.

Both damper and lintel should have the bearing surfaces at each end wrapped in fiberglass wool to allow for heat expansion.

Dampers come with a choice of controls for opening and closing. Some controls extend through the facing, some work by chain, and others have levers operated by a poker.

**Step 14. Finishing the facing.** With the firebox complete and the damper in place, you're ready to build the facing. Be sure to leave 2 inches of air space between both the firebox and facing masonry and the header at the top of the opening. (Check local building codes for clearances required between masonry and any combustible material adjacent to the firebox or flue.)

Among the patterns for finishing mortar joints in facings are flush, weathered, concave, and V-joint. For smooth mortar joints, use a mason's pointing trowel.

Restore the inner wall surface with patching plaster, wallboard, or whatever material matches the existing surface.

Lay the outer hearth to the edges of the subhearth. Fill any gaps with strips of subflooring and add pieces of finish flooring salvaged from that removed when you made the floor opening.

**Step 15. Sealing around the opening.** To make certain that water will not seep into the house around the edges of the fireplace opening, seal all points where masonry passes through the woodwork. Where bricks meet wood framing, they should be laid against felt paper. Around the sides, where masonry meets exterior siding, the joint is flashed or caulked, depending on the type of siding. For stucco walls, use a stucco patch, available at home improvement centers.

Metal flashing is needed across the top of the firebox to divert water away from the opening. Slip one angle of the flashing under the outer wall covering, cover with weatherproof paper, and then nail on the finished covering. The angle of the flashing that fits into the brickwork should be mortared into a running joint and sealed with mastic. Top flashing is shaped to overlap sides.

**Step 13**

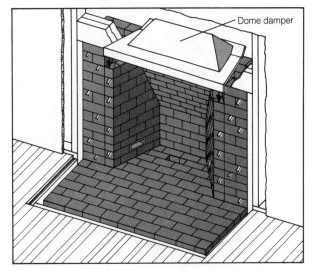

**Step 14**

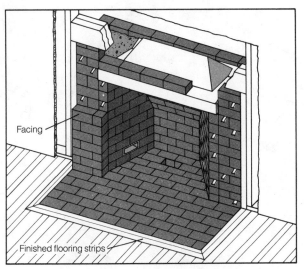

**Step 15**

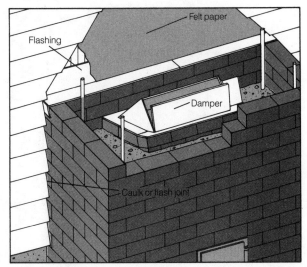

**Step 16**

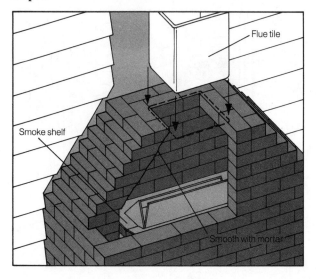

Flue tile

Smoke shelf

Smooth with mortar

**Step 17**

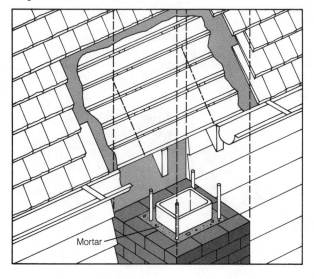

Mortar

**Step 18**

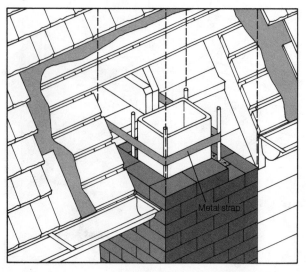

Metal strap

**Step 16. Building the throat and chimney.** Brickwork on both sides of the firebox should be stepped in for six or seven courses until the throat narrows down to flue size. The last course should be laid to provide a ledge just wide enough for the flue tile to rest on.

The sloped inner surface—which forms the smoke dome—should be smoothed with mortar to ease the passage of flue gases and to prevent soot buildup. Mortar used for this job should be slightly richer (more cement, less sand) and drier (less water) than that used for laying brick. Mortar is applied with a square-edged plasterer's trowel. Brick used for the inner surface of the smoke dome should have a textured surface so the mortar will key into it.

Before setting the chimney, fasten weatherproof paper to the house wall where bricks will rest against it. When setting flue tiles, it's more practical to set and cement them in place and then lay the outside bricks around them. (If bricks are laid first, the new masonry is likely to be damaged when the heavy tiles are positioned.) To cut a tile to length, place a cement sack inside, fill tightly with sand, and then sever with a series of chisel cuts.

**Step 17. Penetrating the roof.** At the point where the chimney passes the roof line, it's necessary to cut into the eave in order for the chimney to pass and to install an anchoring device to brace the chimney.

Clear away the roof surfacing material for an area a foot larger all around than the opening needed for the chimney.

Mark cutting lines on the roof sheathing 2 inches wider than each side of the masonry and saw out the pieces. Remove enough of the sheathing so you can freely reach the plate. If the tips of the rafters extend beyond the roof line, cut them off flush with the outside wall. If your house is equipped with gutters, cut them with a hacksaw. (Note the reinforcing steel, required in earthquake country, in each corner of the chimney masonry, sealed in with mortar.)

**Step 18. Tying-in the chimney.** At the point where it passes the roof line, the chimney must be anchored to the framing of the house. There are several ways to do this. The drawing shows one of the most common. A 1-inch iron strap is bent around a tile (and the reinforcing steel, if any), twisted to pass flat through a mortar joint, and nailed to the top plate or to a rafter. If you must fasten the strap to a ceiling joist, nail cross supports across several joists to help distribute the load.

Repair cut gutters by filing off rough edges and soldering caps on each of the end cuts. Be sure to buy caps made of the same metal as the gutters; otherwise, electrolytic reaction between the different metals will corrode the edges and destroy the seal. Make sure, too, that there's a downspout to drain each of the severed gutters.

**Step 19. Fitting the flashing.** Install metal (copper, lead, galvanized iron, or aluminum) flashing around the chimney to seal the opening against water leakage. Flashing is applied in two layers. The bottom layer (B and E in the drawing) is fitted under the roof covering and bent to lie flat against the brickwork. The second layer (A, C, and D in the drawing) is cemented and caulked into the masonry and fitted so it overlaps the first layer. This is known as counter flashing.

Except where they overlap, flashing joints should all be soldered. Allow some leeway between cap and base flashing to permit the chimney to settle or move slightly without rupturing the seal.

In very cold climates, a cricket (shown below) should be substituted for flashing on the up side of the chimney.

**Step 20. Installing a cricket.** In severe winter regions, a cricket, or saddle, is constructed on the up side of the chimney to divert water and snow away from the top side. Snow and ice collecting against a chimney can seriously damage flashing, resulting in a leaky roof. Heavy snow loads may even do structural damage to the masonry itself.

A sizable cricket consists of a ridgeboard and post, sheathed with plywood or 1-inch boards and covered with sheet metal. Crickets for smaller chimneys may be all sheet metal. Metal flanges extend several inches under shingles and up the chimney. Counter flashing covers the joint where the cricket meets the chimney.

You can have the cricket made at a sheet-metal shop at the same time that you order flashing. To install the cricket and counter flashing, follow the alphabetical sequence shown in the illustration at right.

## USING A METAL INSERT

Several manufacturers offer metal inserts for masonry fireplaces. These replace the firebox, smoke dome, and damper, saving the complicated work of building the first two and seating the third. They also assure correct firebox dimensions and shape for efficient draw in the chimney. (Using a prefabricated metal insert replaces Steps 10–13, as well as the corresponding design work.)

Some units are conventional, but a majority are designed to make the fireplace a heat-circulating one. The heat-circulating design shown is a composite of several manufacturers' units. Most inserts incorporate the ducts into the basic shell.

Inserts are available in a range of sizes in both conventional and heat-circulating models. When installed, these units require at least a 1-inch clearance between their outer shells and the surrounding masonry to allow for heat expansion of the metal firebox.

**Step 19**

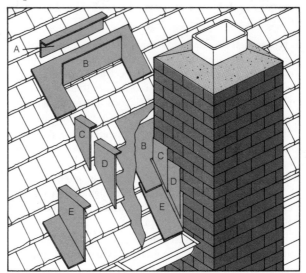

**Step 20**

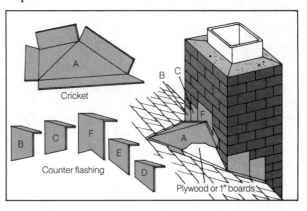

Cricket

Counter flashing

Plywood or 1" boards

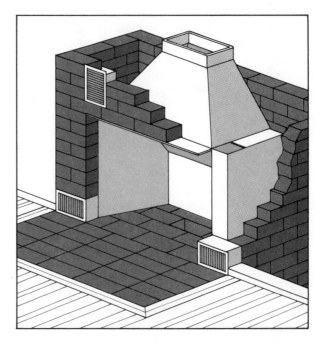

# INSTALLING A FACTORY-BUILT FIREPLACE

A typical factory-built fireplace installation requires neither the credentials of an architect nor the experience of a veteran contractor. Some built-in units call for no more than modest framing skills. But this is not to say there are no problems. Fireplaces built outside a wall and enclosed in a chase may be beyond the skills of the average amateur.

If you do decide to install your own fireplace, the key as always is planning and more planning. A successful job depends on knowing where the fireplace will sit, down to a fraction of an inch, and what will happen inside the wall or above the ceiling as a result of the placement. Success also depends on knowing how much of what kinds of material you'll need to support the fireplace.

Instructions are given here for both inside-the-wall and outside-the-wall building sequences. While you're in the planning stage, look through these pages to gain an understanding of the procedures involved and the available options.

## OPTIONS IN BUILT-IN FIREPLACES

The first decision you'll have to make is between a heat-circulating and a radiant fireplace. Even after you've made this choice, you'll be confronted with dozens of models offering hundreds of options, some of them important to heating efficiency, some of them crucial to a fireplace's capacity to fit into your planned installation, and others important only as esthetic choices.

Some of the options involve air-washed glass enclosures, refractory components, outside air ducting, and heat-recovery systems. As the demand for factory-built fireplaces has increased, manufacturers have responded with a number of innovative designs, including fireplaces with glass doors on two, three, or even all four sides. (For a look at some examples, glance through the chapter that begins on page 15.)

But it's important to remember that a factory-built fireplace is not adaptable to every whim. This is especially true when it's being added to an existing structure. To get the fireplace best suited to your needs, shop as widely as you can. Looking firsthand at what's available is the best teacher, and talking with dealers will raise new questions at every turn.

**Dimensions.** Although factory-built fireplaces come in a wide range of shapes and sizes, typical firebox openings run from 36 to 42 inches wide and 16 to 24 inches high. As noted in the chart on page 59, the size of your room will govern to a considerable degree the size of this opening.

Just as important are the overall dimensions of the fireplace. These will determine—at least in part—whether the fireplace projects fully into the room, is placed entirely outside the wall, or falls somewhere in between. Typical outside dimensions for built-in fireplaces vary from 46 to 52 inches wide, 23 to 26 inches front to back, and 40 to 58 inches from the bottom of the firebox to the top of the smoke dome. In short, there's far more variation in overall size than in firebox opening.

Detailed dimensions may matter even more than overall dimensions if your space is tight. For example, depending on the manufacturer's specifications, the chimney collar may fall at the center of the front-to-back axis, or it may fall off to one side or the other. The exact location of the chimney collar might allow you to run your chimney as planned in a partially projecting fireplace, or it might prohibit you from putting it where you expected.

## Various Duct-placement Designs

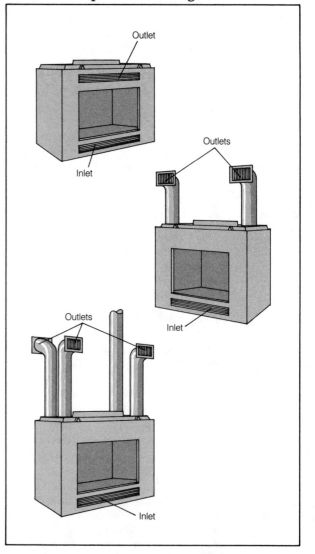

*Variations on the theme of heat circulation are several. Units that expel warmed air at the top of the fireplace opening work best if heat is meant to be kept close to the fireplace; higher outlets send air farther away.*

**Duct placement in heat-circulating fireplaces.** Similar concerns can be raised about duct openings in heat-circulating models, as duct placement varies even more widely than that of chimney collars. (For several different examples, see the illustration on the facing page.)

Warm air rises and cold air sinks, so the first rule of duct placement is simple enough: cold air intakes must be at or near the bottom of the fireplace and warm air outlets at or near the top. Still, manufacturers offer a great variety of placements of both intakes and outlets, and for good reasons.

To decide on the placements that will work best for you requires both a thoughtful appraisal of where you want the warmed air to go and a careful look at how the face of the fireplace will relate to duct openings. This is especially important if you're looking at models with fixed inlets and outlets, but even models with adjustable ducting have some limitations that may make one unit preferable to the others.

For example, it's difficult or impossible to place an outlet vent lower than the point at which the adjustable portion of the ducting leaves the fireplace shell. If you want to get warmed air into the room at the lowest possible elevation in order to get maximum warmth near the fireplace, look for models with relatively low outlets. On the other hand, if you want some of the warmed air to rise into a stairwell or even to be ducted into an upstairs room, you might prefer to look for a unit with ducts placed higher off the floor. (Ducts that will be venting heated air through a combustible wall must be tested to the Underwriter's Laboratory standard for furnaces.)

Some models are designed to take air in from the front and expel it from the sides, or vice versa. In others, all vents are in the front. This can affect the design of your fireplace facing. Corner fireplaces, for example, are easier to frame if all vents are at the front. The same is true for fireplaces set outside a wall.

If you're short of space, you may need a fireplace with ducting and vents incorporated into the shell rather than extending out to each side.

**Forced-air circulation.** If a heat-circulating fireplace is to be located in a large room, you may want to consider low-velocity fans for the ducting. Some circulating systems include these as standard equipment; others offer them as options. The idea is the same as in a forced-air furnace: to mix air evenly rather than let it drift into warmer and cooler layers.

**Outside air for combustion.** The heat efficiency of any fireplace is improved by ducting in combustion air from outside. Weather-tight houses can inhibit draft too much for a fire to burn well, and draft-ridden houses can even experience a net heat loss as the fire sucks outside air in through cracks around doors and windows to feed combustion.

The placement of such an inlet in a built-in fireplace can be crucial. In some models, the duct is in the firebox floor, so it must reach down into a crawl space or basement. In others, paired ducts at the sides are flexible, so they can reach down through the floor or out through a wall; these add several inches to the width of framing.

**Firebox lining.** Most firebox floors are lined with fireclay or another refractory material. Some linings are patterned to look like brick; others are smooth.

The functional difference is when you get warmed, not how much. The refractory material slows the convection process at first, but, once heated, it keeps warming air even after the fire dwindles.

**Knockout for gas jets.** If you plan to have a gas log lighter, placement of the knockouts can be a factor, especially if you'll have to work in cramped space or if you plan a partial projection of the fireplace. Most units have knockouts on both side walls.

**Weight.** Fireplace units alone weigh between 150 and 700 pounds. The chimneys used on most factory-built units weigh about 8 pounds per lineal foot. (These chimneys meet similar requirements as Class A chimneys, but they're an integral part of the factory-built fireplace and are generally larger than the conventional Class A chimneys.) For each type of factory-built fireplace, manufacturers are required to list all acceptable chimney brands and minimum clearances.

**Support.** Factory-built fireplaces must be placed on hard, noncombustible flooring.

Outside chase systems, if cantilevered from the wall of the house, should be constructed as part of the joist structure of the house. This will prevent future sagging and cracking of the chimney, which can reduce the efficiency of the fireplace and present a potential fire hazard.

## INSTALLATION GUIDELINES

Where you put the fireplace in relation to a wall—or walls— does much to govern the size of the job.

As shown in the drawing on page 58, the basic choices are to place the fireplace inside a wall or to fit it through a wall. If you place the unit inside a wall, you'll lose a maximum of interior space, but you'll only have to cut through the ceiling and roof for passage of the chimney. On the other hand, if you fit the fireplace through an outside wall, you'll have to open the wall and probably cut through an eave, but you'll be repaid in saved space. (Instructions for this type of installation begin on page 91.) Fitting the fireplace into an interior wall is a possibility if you have space to spare in an adjoining room.

In addition to structural alterations, you must add framing to cover the sides and back of the fireplace and part or all of the chimney. Interior framing is less critical than exterior work because it doesn't have to withstand weathering and requires no foundation. Another advantage of interior installation is better heat and a stronger draft. Also, there's no smoky odor when the fireplace is not in use, as can be the case with exterior installations.

Once you've made your basic site selection, you'll need to pinpoint fireplace placement with your specific structural limitations in mind. Most of these are obstructions to passage of the chimney. Designs are available that will allow you to run the chimney inside or outside, or, by offsetting it to pass through a wall, some of each.

## ESTIMATING BUILDING MATERIALS

To get a clear picture of how much a fireplace will cost, you'll need to make an estimate of building materials.

Framing lumber for the fireplace and raised hearth is usually 2 by 4s for studs and for top and sole plates. In most cases, framing inside the house is covered by ⅜-inch wallboard or plywood if the final facing is to be masonry. Facing also may match existing interior walls.

For a fireplace installed inside, headers at openings in the ceilings and roof should match existing joists and rafters. If extra support is required under the floor, this support, too, should match existing members.

For fireplaces installed outside an exterior wall, headers for opened walls must be made of 2 by 6s. The chase enclosing the fireplace and chimney must have a masonry foundation and conventional 2 by 4 stud walls. Chases are usually covered to match exterior walls, but they may be faced with simulated masonry or masonry veneer. Most chases are insulated all or in part with fiberglass batts to protect the fireplace against heat loss.

## MEASURING FOR A CHIMNEY

To estimate your needs, first make an elevation sketch of your house similar to the one above, at right. As shown, measure the height of the fireplace room (A), the room above, if any (B), and the attic from the proposed ceiling opening to the high side of the roof opening (C).

Next, figure the chimney height above the roof. The chimney must extend at least 3 feet above the high side of the roof opening and must be 2 feet taller than the highest point on the roof. It should extend at least 12 feet above the firebox. The highest point may be a ridge, dormer, or cupola; on steep-pitched roofs, the point may fall on the roof plane itself. To get the total height, add the above-roof height to measurements A, B, and C, plus the thicknesses of the ceilings and roof.

To determine the amount of chimney pipe needed, subtract from your original total the height of the fireplace and that of a raised hearth, if you're using one. Note any offsets.

This information will allow your fireplace dealer to help you estimate your chimney material requirements. (A reminder: You'll probably need variable lengths of pipe for the safest, sturdiest chimney; consult your dealer for details.)

## Measuring for a Chimney

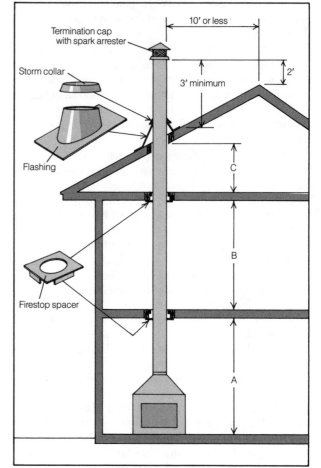

## TOOLS

Framing tools include a hammer and saw, a carpenter's square, a spirit level, a plumb line, a drill and bits, slot and Phillips screwdrivers, and a good measuring tape.

For masonry work, the basic tools are a trowel, a float, and a brick set or tile cutter, plus a mixing bucket.

## INSTALLING A BUILT-IN INSIDE A WALL

The following sequence shows a typical installation. It's meant only as a general planning guide to help you understand the process and decide if you want to do the job yourself or hire someone to do it for you. Your fireplace manufacturer will provide detailed instructions.

**Step 1. Locating and preparing the hearth.** With the fireplace location precisely established and marked, the hearth site must be prepared before you put the fireplace into position. You have three options: a raised hearth, a hearth flush with the floor, or a hearth laid over a finished floor.

For a raised hearth, frame a platform over the finished floor. The technique shown for the vertical sections is the same as for a stud wall. Use ¾-inch plywood for the platform. Place a 24-gauge galvanized steel or aluminum sheet under the firebox, extending it to the end of the hearth.

Reinforce the platform with 2 by 4 cross members centered beneath joints in the plywood. Remember that the bottom thickness of the firebox of a factory-built fireplace can range from 6 to 9 inches, so the opening will be noticeably higher than the hearth extension unless you set the fireplace on a separate, lower platform.

For a hearth extension flush with the finished floor, cut away the floor to the desired width and length. The noncombustible hearth materials must be at least ⅜ inch thick and be without a break; they also must cover a code-required minimum area. Most finished floors are ⅜ inch or thicker, but almost none is thick enough to allow the inner and outer hearths to meet flush.

For a hearth laid over a finished floor, no carpentry is required, but note that such hearths produce a toe-stubbing lip, and thick ones may obstruct the inlets of a heat-circulating fireplace. Depending on the hearth material you use, you may have to lay down sheet metal underneath. Consult your local building code.

When you're planning your outer hearth, remember that for fireplaces with an opening of 6 square feet or less, the hearth must extend a minimum of 8 inches to each side and 16 inches to the front of the opening. For fireplaces with openings greater than 6 square feet, the hearth must extend no less than 12 inches to each side of the fireplace opening and 20 inches in front of it. Since requirements vary, consult your building department and the manufacturer's instructions. Manufacturers often offer factory-produced hearths made of decorative tile, stone, brick, or other materials that will meet code.

Do not lay the outer hearth at this time.

Move the fireplace into its exact position. Secure it against movement with temporary blocks nailed at each side and—if the fireplace stands away from the wall—at each rear corner.

## Step 2. Locating and cutting the ceiling opening.
To find the center of the ceiling opening for a vertical chimney, plumb to the center of the fireplace chimney collar as shown. If the chimney is to be offset, plumb as shown; then use the formula provided by the manufacturer to transfer the center point.

The opening is cut square, with two sides parallel to the ceiling joists; it must be 4 inches wider than the diameter of the chimney pipe. If you're working into an unfloored attic, the single opening is enough. If you're working toward a floor above, you'll have to cut through it. You can cut either a matching square hole or a circle 4 inches larger in diameter than the chimney. In this case, mark the center of the top opening by drilling through both ceiling and floor.

**Step 1**

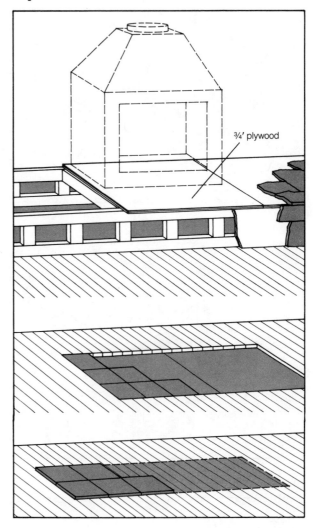

¾' plywood

**Step 2**

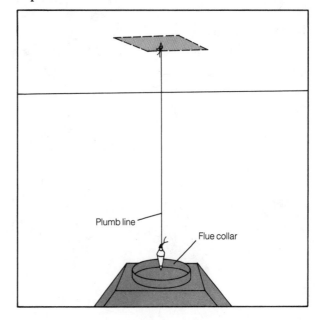

Plumb line

Flue collar

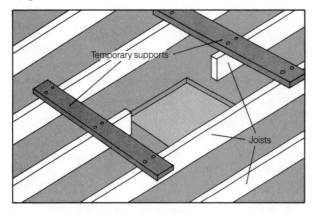

Temporary supports

Joists

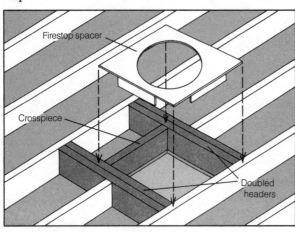

Firestop spacer

Crosspiece

Doubled
headers

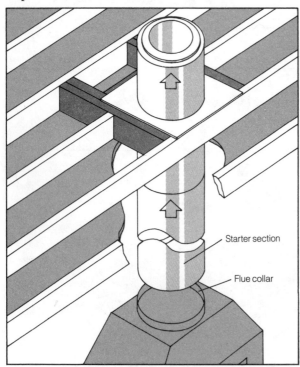

Starter section

Flue collar

**Step 3. Framing the ceiling opening.** With an opening for the chimney cut in the ceiling, one joist will usually obstruct the opening. If so, and you're working into an unfloored attic, work from above.

First, tack temporary supports across the joist to be trimmed and its neighbors on either side. Then trim out the joist that obstructs the opening, allowing room for doubled headers at each side. Using the same dimension lumber as the joists, install the doubled headers. You can nail into the ends or toenail them. Either way, use at least two nails at each end of each header, and two more to secure the trimmed joist end. Add single crosspieces to make a square frame around the opening.

If there's a finished floor above or if you're working toward a flat roof with no crawl space between it and the ceiling, you won't have to brace before you trim the obstructing joist. But you will have to enlarge the ceiling opening to accommodate the doubled headers and crosspieces. Fit the headers from below, toenailing them into place; then add the crosspieces. (On occasion, you may be able to nail from the roof, but avoid the temptation to make this the larger opening; it will make flashing more difficult to install.)

**Step 4. Installing firestop spacers.** A firestop spacer assures that the manufacturer's specified clearance between the chimney and combustibles is met whenever a chimney penetrates a ceiling or floor. It also provides lateral support for the chimney. A spacer must be used every time a chimney penetrates a ceiling or floor. Standard firestop spacers can be used when the chimney penetrates the ceiling or floor at a 90° angle, but special firestop spacers must be installed when the chimney penetrates at an angle of 15° or 30°. If you can work from above, install the firestop spacer on top of the ceiling joists. If you don't have access, nail it to the bottom edges of the joists.

**Step 5. Assembling the chimney sections.** Chimney sections designed for factory-built fireplaces come in two basic designs: a double- or triple-wall air-cooled design and a double-wall insulated chimney. Air-cooled chimneys dissipate their heat through air-flow chambers between each wall. Insulated chimneys have solid insulation between the two walls and contain the heat within the flue area.

Most fireplace manufacturers provide a special starter section that locks into the collar at the top of the fireplace. The male end of the pipe is installed downward. Above this, regular sections fit together either by a snap-lock method or by a twist-and-lock motion. It's very important that each section be locked firmly into place.

The upper ends of each chimney section are usually marked with an arrow or the word "up" to avoid any chance of the chimney being installed upside down. Assemble the chimney upward only until it extends just slightly beyond the firestop spacer or the flashing. Be sure to maintain the necessary clearances. Don't combine elbows to incline the chimney more than 30° from vertical; this will seriously hamper chimney function.

**Step 6. Locating and cutting the roof opening.** The process for locating the center point of the roof opening is exactly the same as that shown for finding a ceiling opening (see Step 2 on page 87), except that you plumb to the center of the chimney section where it extends above the firestop spacer. If the chimney run is straight, drive a nail through the roof to mark the point. If you plan to offset the chimney, use the manufacturer's formula to locate the center.

Measure and mark the opening from atop the roof. On a pitched roof, the opening may have to be oblong-shaped to provide the proper clearances as specified by the manufacturer. Cut from on top of the roof.

**Step 7. Framing the roof opening.** When rafters are spaced 16 inches on center, the process is very similar to framing the ceiling opening, except that where a roof rafter must be trimmed, temporary braces are tacked on from the underside. Use doubled headers made of the same dimension lumber as the rafters to support each end of the trimmed rafter, and single members to frame the remaining sides.

If your rafters are spaced more than 16 inches on center, you may be able to avoid trimming one, although it's possible you'll need to make an offset with a pair of elbows. (In planning, you may want to locate the offset between the fireplace and the ceiling, where there's usually more room to maneuver than there is in the attic. Obviously, it's too late to do this after the ceiling opening has been cut and framed.)

No firestop spacer is required at the roof; flashing takes its place.

**Step 8. Installing flashing and the storm collar.** Manufacturers differ in their approach to flashing. Some require that it be installed before the chimney is extended upward through the roof opening; others use designs that can be placed after the chimney pokes through the roof. Most often, it's a matter of how the flashing fits under the roofing. In any event, carefully follow the installation instructions provided by the manufacturer.

Once the flashing is in place and the chimney extended above it, place the storm collar over the chimney pipe and push it down snugly against the flashing. Seal the joint between the storm collar and chimney pipe.

Note: This instruction assumes the chimney will remain exposed above the roof. If you choose to enclose it, check with your building department for code requirements on framing and other construction details.

**Step 9. Installing the cap and bracing.** Chimney caps are usually included with most factory-built chimney assemblies. Be sure to choose a cap recommended for use with your chimney design. A poorly fitting cap can seriously hamper chimney efficiency.

Chimneys extending 5 feet or more above the roof may require bracing. Check the manufacturer's specifications or consult your building department.

**Steps 6 & 7**

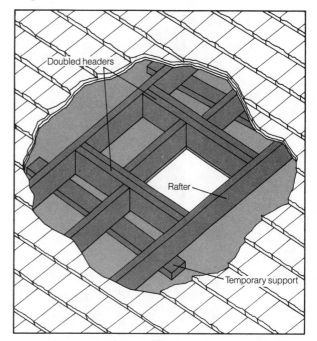

Doubled headers

Rafter

Temporary support

**Steps 8 & 9**

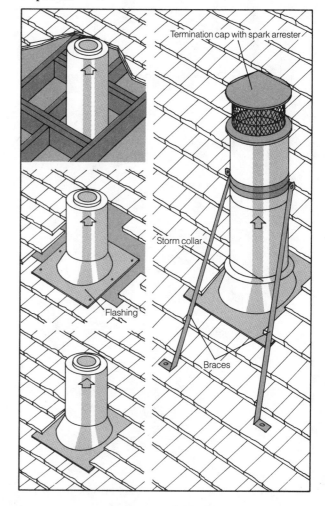

Termination cap with spark arrester

Storm collar

Flashing

Braces

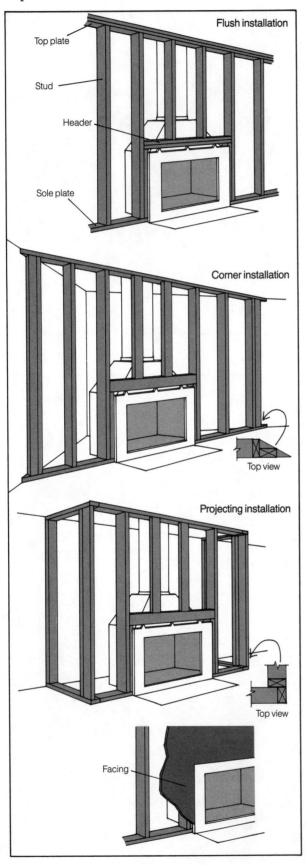

Flush installation

Top plate

Stud

Header

Sole plate

Corner installation

Top view

Projecting installation

Top view

Facing

**Step 10. Framing in the fireplace.** Enclose the fireplace as you would frame a conventional wall. Although typically this means using 2 by 4s for sole and top plates and 2 by 4s spaced 16 inches on center for studs, be sure to consult the manufacturer's instructions for specifications. Using the wrong size headers, for example, can actually cause a fire.

If you're installing a heat-circulating fireplace with flexible ducting, you'll have to frame openings for inlets and/or outlets. You may want to make a trial assembly of the ducts before framing begins to make sure they'll fit the framing without problems. Also, before you begin to frame, cut the opening for an outside combustion air duct and plumb the gas line for a gas lighter if you're using these optional devices.

The framing members must be set back from the front edge of the firebox opening so that facing materials will fit. If you'll leave the fireplace face frame exposed, set the studs back far enough for the facing to fit flush with the frame. (For example, if you're using ⅜-inch wallboard, set the framing ⅜ inch behind the face frame. If you plan to cover the wall framing with standard brick, the offset must equal the brick plus ⅜ inch for the wallboard or plywood skin covering the framing plus the thickness of the mortar between brick and skin.)

Be sure the fireplace is secured in place so it doesn't shift later on. Check that your installation conforms to the manufacturer's guidelines for air-space clearances to combustibles on the top and sides. Factory-built fireplaces have stand-offs and V-shaped spacing tabs on the firebox to maintain clearances. Framing members may not be notched to fit these in. (Don't be misled by the term "zero clearance," commonly used in the past to describe factory-built fireplaces. Most are zero clearance only at the base, not on the top or sides.)

**Step 11. Facing the fireplace.** Two basic rules apply when you're facing the fireplace. First, if your facing will be made of plywood, wallboard, or any other combustible material, it must not cover the fireplace face frame. Instead, you will have to butt it flush against the outer edges of the frame or, if it's to project forward beyond the face frame, set it at least 6 inches from the sides of the firebox opening and 12 inches above the top. This requirement also applies to mantels.

Second, if you're using a particularly heavy facing material, such as stone or adobe blocks, you may have to reinforce the flooring beneath. Consult your local building department for specifics. For information on working with masonry, see the *Sunset* book *Basic Masonry Illustrated*.

**Step 12. Finishing the outer hearth.** The outer hearth must be covered with a noncombustible material at least ⅜ inch thick. It must be continuous: tile must be grouted, brick mortared. You can lay masonry loose only if you underlay it with 24-gauge sheet metal.

If the flooring underneath the fireplace is combustible, you must include a metal sealing strip (follow the manufacturer's specifications). This seals the crack between the fireplace and the outer hearth to prevent sparks and ash from igniting the flooring.

## INSTALLING A BUILT-IN OUTSIDE A WALL

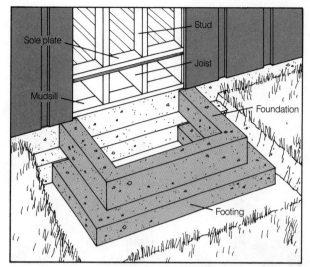

Common building practice dictates that outside fireplace installations be enclosed completely within a chase, a sort of room without windows or doors. The chase both protects and hides the metal firebox and chimney. A chase can narrow above the fireplace and be covered to resemble a masonry chimney, or it can extend in an unbroken line to the top and be covered to match the siding of the house. In either case, adding the framing to an existing building is complex. Skilled amateurs can do the work, but most home owners prefer to hire a contractor.

The following sequence describes a typical installation, but it's only a guide to planning, not an instruction.

**Step 1. Building the foundation.** Measure and dig out the site to receive a continuous footing and foundation of the same size as that of your house. To meet typical building codes, the foundation will have steel reinforcing bars not only within itself but also tying it to the existing foundation. Top the foundation with a mudsill. (Typically, the mudsill will be flush with its counterpart in the main foundation, but the foundation is one opportunity to control the height of the platform on which the fireplace will rest. See Step 3.)

**Step 2. Opening the wall.** First, cut away both interior and exterior wall surface materials. Next, erect a support reaching from floor to ceiling and beyond each side of the opening. (This supports the ceiling joists once you cut the wall studs. For more information, see Step 4 on page 78.)

With the ceiling support in place, trim the wall studs blocking the opening. Nail in a doubled header of 2 by 6s; then add two jack studs at each side. Once the jack studs are in place, trim the sole plate if you're planning an outer hearth flush with the inside finished floor, the usual case in this space-saving installation.

**Step 3. Framing the platform.** The illustration for this step assumes a platform flush with the subfloor, permitting a ⅜-inch-thick outer hearth that will be flush with the finished floor. In this case, you can overlap, or plate, joists for the platform with existing joists in your subfloor. To plate, overlap the extension joist at least a foot along the existing floor joist; then secure it with at least three nails at each end of the overlap. It's best to nail from both sides.

If you plan to change level (in order to have a raised hearth or to lower the fireplace so the firebox floor is flush with the outer hearth), consult your building department before designing a foundation and joist system. Especially in cases of lowering a firebox, you risk violating codes on minimum clearances of wood from earth and wood from firebox opening.

**Step 3**

**Step 5**

**Step 6**

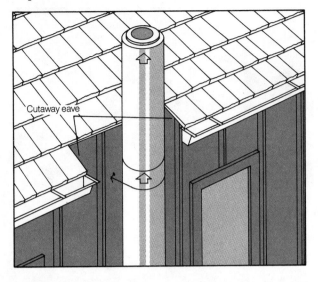

Cutaway eave

**Step 7**

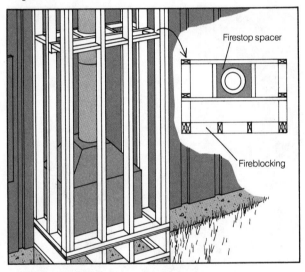

Firestop spacer

Fireblocking

**Steps 8 & 9**

Insulation

**Step 4. Positioning the fireplace.** With the platform complete, slide the fireplace into position; then add a sole plate around the platform perimeter.

**Step 5. Assembling the chimney.** Chimney sections lock together. Because the diameter of your pipe may be too large to fit between studs set 16 inches on center, assemble it at least to eave height before you begin to frame. It's a good idea to hold the pipe in place with temporary wire bands while you frame. Pipes of smaller diameters can be assembled now or after framing is complete.

**Step 6. Cutting the eave.** To accommodate the framing for the chase, cut the eave line back flush with the house wall and just wide enough to accept the framing with its covering. (For a more complete description of this step, see Steps 17 and 18 on page 82.)

**Step 7. Framing the chase.** This is a difficult task for many amateur carpenters. The basics are straightforward enough: use 2 by 4 studs to the desired height, spacing them 16 inches on center and anchoring them to sole and top plates. Diagonal bracing may be required by code, but this is simple, too. The complications arise in securing the studs butted against the existing wall to framing members inside that wall, in narrowing the chase if this is part of the design, and in installing flashing where the side walls of the chase meet the existing walls of the house. If you're not familiar with the techniques, seek professional advice.

Another area of some complexity is fireblocking. One fireblock is required for every 8 feet of vertical rise. These fireblocks must form a solid horizontal stop across the chase to block upward drafts, and the chimney must have a firestop spacer where it passes through the fireblock, as in inside installations. Our drawing approximates the framing for a code-approved firestop, but be sure to check with your building inspector before designing your chase. The horizontal cover is usually made of ⅝-inch plywood. (The cover is not shown in the drawing; it must fit snugly against the walls of the chase on all four sides, meeting firestop blocks set between the studs.)

**Step 8. Closing the chase and capping the chimney.** When the chase reaches its full height, install a closing (prefabricated sheet-metal closures are usually available in several sizes from fireplace dealers). Then cap the chimney itself, using a termination cap matched to the chimney design.

**Step 9. Insulating and covering the chase.** Chases should be insulated, preferably with unfaced batts sheathed inside wallboard. In mild climates, the insulation need enclose only the fireplace; in cold-winter areas, the whole chase should be insulated. The covering can match the house or simulate masonry.

**Step 10. Framing and facing the fireplace.** The options here are many. For more information, see Steps 10 and 11 on page 90.

# INSTALLING A FREESTANDING METAL FIREPLACE

Of all the types of fireplaces, freestanding models are the easiest to install. You move the unit in, place it on a non-combustible hearth, install the chimney, and then connect the fireplace to the chimney with stove pipe.

## OPTIONS IN FREESTANDING FIREPLACES

Even after you take into account all the different shapes, freestanding fireplaces come in a surprising variety of designs. Some closely resemble wood stoves. Others, heat-circulating models, look just like their built-in cousins. Most are modern designs with almost as much decorative as practical value.

**Finishes.** A majority of freestanding fireplaces are finished in enamel or porcelain enamel, with every color in the spectrum represented. Careful selection of shape and color is imperative, since, unlike with other fireplaces, you can't add the facing of your choice.

**Dimensions.** Heights of freestanding fireplaces are as variable as their shapes. Some globular models reach only 30 to 35 inches above the floor; on the other hand, extreme conical designs can rise as high as 90 inches. Average height ranges between 40 and 45 inches.

Diameters of globes or cylinders run from 24 to 48 inches, as do widths of stovelike rectangular models. The smaller types take wood logs up to 20 inches long; larger ones will accept 27- to 30-inch logs.

**Weight.** Typical units weigh in the range of 140 to 150 pounds. Lightweights go as low as 90 pounds; heavyweights approach 400. The reason for the generally light weights of freestanding fireplaces is that typical units have single metal walls to enhance radiation. Heat-circulating models, however, are heavier since they have double walls, ducting, and other extras.

Many single-wall models come without a refractory liner in place in the firebox. In this case, the unit comes with a bag of dry fireclay. Home owners mix their own mortar and form their own lining, following the manufacturer's directions.

**Heat-circulating fireplaces.** A few freestanding fireplace units circulate heated air through a ducting system. In some models, the inlet is in the pedestal and the outlet is across the top of the firebox opening. In other units, the inlet is located at the rear and the outlet located on either side of the firebox opening. Some also have small fans to force air circulation.

You may also find freestanding fireplaces with ducts to bring in combustion air from outside. (Only fireplaces with this capability are approved for use in mobile homes.)

## ADDING A FREESTANDING FIREPLACE

Installing the fireplace itself is easy, compared to putting in a masonry fireplace. Instructions provided by the fireplace manufacturer include hearth requirements, recommended distances between the fireplace and combustible surfaces, and details on chimney installation.

A few freestanding metal fireplaces are so constructed that they can be placed close to combustible materials; clearance distances required for other models range widely, so be sure to consult the manufacturer's specifications.

All freestanding fireplaces must have floor hearths to protect combustible floors from flying sparks and embers. Hearths can be made of almost any noncombustible material, although brick, tile, and stone are most often used. Attractive hearth designs for freestanding metal fireplaces appear in the chapter beginning on page 15.

Prefabricated metal chimneys for these fireplaces can be installed through the wall or ceiling, as shown in the illustration below. The chimney and its components must be safety-tested by Underwriter's Laboratories (UL) and approved for use by local codes.

Installing a hearth and chimney for a freestanding fireplace is the same as the procedure used for a wood stove. For help, see the instructions in the chapter beginning on page 97.

If your house has an existing, unused flue, you can probably use it, but you may have to reline the chimney (for help, see page 106).

### Connecting a Freestanding Fireplace to a Chimney

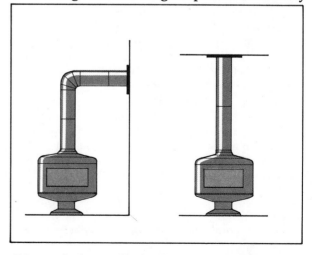

*Chimneys for freestanding fireplaces begin either at a wall (at left) or in a ceiling (at right).*

# FIREPLACE SAFETY, MAINTENANCE & USE

There's more to a cozy fire than just setting the logs ablaze. You'll need to add some chimney and fireplace safety procedures to your talents, as well as some fire-building and maintenance techniques.

## DEALING WITH CREOSOTE

When moisture expelled from burning wood combines with combustible gases escaping unburned up the chimney flue, creosote is formed. This messy, tarry substance, an almost unavoidable by-product of wood combustion, is one of the biggest problems facing a fireplace—or wood stove—owner.

If layers of creosote are allowed to build up on the flue lining, the draft will be restricted and the creosote will bake on, becoming brittle and shiny. This deposit is highly flammable; if it's not removed on a regular basis, a chimney fire may result.

**Why creosote forms.** Creosote builds up inside the chimney when flue temperatures are low; this allows the substance to stick to the lining. Wood burners that send a lot of heat up their flues will not make much creosote because their flue temperatures are likely to be too high for creosote deposits to form, even if creosote is present in the flue gases.

Creosote collects most heavily in the coolest portions of the flue; in most installations, this will be near the top of the chimney. Metal chimneys may have fewer problems with creosote than masonry ones since their relatively higher rate of thermal expansion and contraction tends to fracture creosote deposits, causing them to flake away and fall back into the fire.

**Taking preventive measures.** To avoid excess creosote, make sure you burn only seasoned wood. Use softwoods, such as pine, only to augment seasoned hardwoods, like oak and hickory. Hardwoods produce far less creosote than softwoods, but adding some well-seasoned pine or cedar to a hardwood fire can make it burn hotter, resulting in less creosote adhering to the chimney.

Inspect your chimney and connecting pipes at least twice a year during the burning season and clean them if necessary. Plan to clean the flue at least once a year—more often if your fireplace is used regularly. (For instructions on cleaning a chimney and fireplace, see page 96.) Creosote is a part of wood heating, but it need not be a hazard.

## USING YOUR FIREPLACE SAFELY

Regardless of the type of fireplace, having an enjoyable fire will require some effort. Laying a good fire—one that starts easily and burns evenly—takes practice. With experience, you'll develop a knack for feeding the fire to maintain an even burning rate.

For fuel, wood is still the favorite. It's affordable and widely available. (For help in choosing which wood to burn, see page 9.) Composition logs, available at many supermarkets, are sometimes chemically treated to provide colorful flames; these relatively inexpensive logs will burn for 2 to 3 hours. However, do not burn them in combination with other fuels; follow the manufacturer's instructions carefully.

## LAYING A GOOD FIRE

First, check to be sure that the fireplace damper is open. (It's best to keep it closed between fires to minimize heat loss from the house.) Lay the logs on a grate (shown below) or on andirons to allow air to reach the fire from below. Without these, you'll have to use a pair of green logs to elevate the wood from the fireplace floor.

Next, put several crumpled or twisted sheets of newspaper in the center of the fireplace; then crisscross several sticks of kindling (preferably a seasoned softwood, such as pine) on top of the paper. Kindling should be split to one-

### How to Make a Fire

*To lay a fire, place crumpled newspaper on a grate, add crisscrossed kindling, and then top with three small logs. Place logs split sides down, one over other two.*

or two-finger lengths. Place three fairly small logs over the kindling, one on top of the other two. Place the logs split sides down, since the split sides will catch faster than the bark sides. These three logs will confine the heat to the center of the fireplace, with each radiating heat to the others. They should not be stacked so tightly that the fire can't escape upward and burn evenly.

Just before lighting the fire, start a good updraft by holding a lighted twist of newspaper high in the throat of the fireplace. (Protect your hands with fire-resistant gloves.) Then bring it down and use it to ignite the paper underneath the kindling.

If the fireplace lets smoke into the room, open a window so that the fire can draw in more air to sustain an updraft.

Placing a large log at the back of the fire, with smaller logs toward the front, will help radiate heat into the room. If the room tends to overheat, build a smaller fire behind a large log placed near the front of the andirons.

If your fireplace is equipped with glass doors, shut them as soon as the paper catches fire. This will help increase the draft and keep any smoke from entering the room. If you only have a firescreen, close it unless you're watching the fire closely and you're burning hardwood that doesn't throw sparks.

Always keep a fire extinguisher nearby. Avoid burning trash or anything other than paper and wood in the fireplace. In many areas, burning trash in a fireplace is illegal. It also can result in an increased buildup of creosote in the chimney.

## FIREPLACE ACCESSORIES

Certain tools made specifically for fireplaces are very useful for starting, managing, and cleaning up after the fire. Often, these tools, which may occupy a place of honor beside your fireplace opening, are decorative as well as utilitarian. In the chapter beginning on page 15, you'll find many examples of attractive and useful fireplace tools.

To start the fire, you can use a special fire lighter, long matches (available in decorative holders) made especially for fireplaces, or a gas-fired log lighter. Andirons or a grate will hold logs off the fireplace floor.

Glass doors provide important protection against flying embers and safeguard children and pets. Some states now require that masonry and factory-built fireplaces be fitted with them. If your fireplace is not equipped with glass doors, they can be retrofitted to most masonry fireplaces. Otherwise, use a protective screen or spark guard.

Tongs and pokers are useful in working the fire and moving logs. Small decorative shovels and brooms are helpful in ash cleanup. It's wise to have a pair of fire-resistant gloves on hand, not only to prevent burns but also to keep you from getting splinters while handling the wood. To carry and hold a fuel supply, you can use a canvas log carrier, a large basket, a stoneware crock, a log crib, or a metal log carrier on wheels. For cleanup, you'll find a shovel and a broom or brush indispensable.

Standard fireplace tools are available in standing or wall-mounted sets that usually contain a shovel, tongs, poker, and brush.

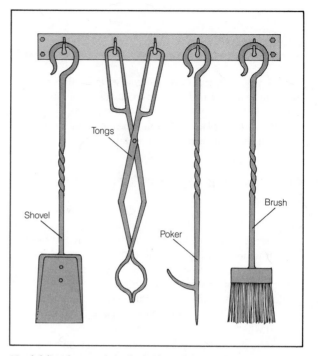

*Useful fireplace tools include (from left) a shovel for scooping ash, tongs for moving logs, a poker for working a fire, and a brush for cleanup.*

## CURING A SMOKY FIREPLACE

If your chimney installation meets all the requirements and still doesn't draw properly, you'll need to do a little detective work to pinpoint the cause.

Sometimes, surrounding hills or tall trees nearby can result in down drafts that bring smoke into the room. A metal chimney cap—stationary or rotating—may be all you need to cure the problem.

Forced-air furnaces, kitchen fans, or doors opposite the fireplace opening can pull smoke from the fireplace into the room. Remedies you'll want to consider for these problems are installing a draft inducer (a fan that draws hot air up and out the flue), turning the fans off, and installing a solid room divider between the door and fireplace.

During spring, birds have been known to build nests in chimneys, a practice that—like beehives or drifting autumn leaves—can have smoky results. Check for such obstructions by lowering a light on an extension cord down the chimney. Adding a chimney cap, like the one shown on page 7, can prevent such occurrences.

If all the causes of smoke have been eliminated and the problem persists, it may be due to faulty construction of the fireplace. In this case, a professional should be consulted. It's possible that the fireplace opening is too large for the flue area. If so, you'll have to decrease the size of the opening; one way to do this is to raise the hearth. An easier solution, and perhaps the best one, is to install a firebox insert, a factory-built steel addition that slips into an existing firebox.

## GOOD MAINTENANCE PRACTICES

As with any other area of your home, your fireplace must be carefully maintained, both to ensure optimum performance and to prevent a dangerous chimney fire. The more you use your fireplace, the more attention you'll have to give to maintaining it in a safe condition.

## CLEANING THE CHIMNEY & FIREPLACE

The only way you can prevent the dangerous buildup of creosote inside your chimney is to clean it regularly. You can have the job done professionally by a local chimney sweep or do it yourself. To find a professional, look in the Yellow Pages under "Chimney Cleaning & Repairing." Chimney sweeps, who often wear the traditional black garb of their predecessors, have the equipment needed to survey the inside of your chimney for creosote buildup and can remove it when needed.

If you decide to do the job yourself, you won't need the top hat of a traditional chimney sweep, but you will need a sweep's steel brush (shown below) if yours is a masonry chimney. Chains, bags of rocks, or other heavy implements are not recommended; they can damage your flue and aren't as effective as a good steel brush. The job is messy, but it shouldn't be intimidating unless your chimney is very long or your roof steeply pitched.

### A Selection of Brushes

*Chimney-sweeping brushes come in a variety of shapes.*

Before you begin, cover all openings with newspaper and masking tape; cover furniture close to the chimney opening with large drop cloths. Be sure to protect your eyes and mouth by wearing a dust mask.

**Cleaning techniques.** To clean the flue, attach the brush to fiberglass rods (the rods snap together in sections—use as many as you need for the length of your chimney). From the roof, lower the brush and rods into the flue, pushing and pulling in short strokes (the brush should fit snugly in the flue). Continue until the brush is down as far as it will go. Then pull it up. Repeat if necessary. Clean the smoke dome from below.

Most of the creosote and soot from the flue will fall onto the smoke shelf. To clean it, take the hose from a heavy-duty vacuum cleaner and reach it behind the damper. You can also use the vacuum for cleaning out the hearth. Don't try to use your household vacuum—the ashes and soot will ruin the motor.

To clean stovepipe sections, dismantle them and carry them outside; clean them carefully with a nylon brush. Check your flue thoroughly with a flashlight to be sure it's clean and then reassemble the stovepipe.

## ASHES, ASHES

Even if you're burning highly seasoned wood, ashes will build up in the firebox over time. The best way to remove them is to use a metal shovel. Avoid using a broom, except for touch-ups; vigorous sweeping will only send a cloud of fine ash through the room.

The most important thing to remember about ash removal is to put the ashes in a fireproof container. Embers can smoulder for days inside an ash pile, even if you haven't had a fire for some time. Use a metal container to store the ashes until you're sure all embers are extinguished. Never place ashes in paper bags set in or near the house. The embers will burn through the bag and ignite the structure.

Some people use fireplace ashes to enhance the soil in garden areas. Hardwood ashes do contain a lot of potash, but they're also highly alkaline. Check your soil conditions before using them. Ashes can also be disposed of in the trash—after you're quite certain there are no more embers. It's best to place the ashes in a metal garbage can.

## REMOVING SMOKE STAINS

Smoke stains on masonry can be removed with a solution of ½ pound trisodium phosphate dissolved in a gallon of water. Wear gloves and apply the solution with a scrub brush.

For stubborn stains, muriatic acid will often do the job, but the acid may discolor bricks. Never use it on stone. The mixture should be 1 part acid to 10 parts water. Mix the solution in a wide-mouthed jar, pouring the water in first and then adding the acid. Apply it with a cloth and immediately rinse it off with water.

# WOOD STOVE INSTALLATION, MAINTENANCE & USE

*Selecting the wood stove that best meets your needs is just the first step in your venture into the world of wood heat. Just as important as choosing the right kind of stove is knowing how to install it, maintain it, and use it correctly and safely.*

*Chimney and hearth installation is not difficult, but it's imperative that the job be done properly to ensure the safe and efficient operation of your wood stove. That means following the specifications of your stove manufacturer and local building code to the letter. Read through the information and procedures described in this chapter to decide if installing your stove is a job better entrusted to an experienced professional or one you want to tackle yourself. You'll find detailed information on required clearances, on locating the stove and chimney, and on assembling the chimney and installing the hearth.*

*Once your stove is in place, ensure its safe operation by careful maintenance and use. Safety tips and upkeep information appear at the end of the chapter, along with a guide to choosing and chopping wood.*

# INSTALLING A WOOD STOVE

Stove, hearth, and chimney constitute the triad of stove installation, the latter two comprising the bulk of work involved. You have the option of tackling one, two, or all three of these phases: installing the chimney, building or purchasing a factory-built hearth, or simply placing the stove on a professionally built hearth and connecting it to the chimney.

The following pages serve as a practical guide for planning and executing each phase of stove installation.

## WHO INSTALLS THE STOVE?

Proper installation of a stove's hearth and chimney can be tricky and often is best left to a professional. A reputable stove installer will be familiar with local building codes and installation practices. Also, the installer can secure the necessary permits, estimate materials, and help you plan a safe, efficient installation.

Some stove manufacturers will not guarantee their products unless they're installed by a professional. Others can be installed by home owners as long as clearance and construction specifications are met. Read through the instructions on the following pages to determine whether or not you want to install the system yourself. If you decide to tackle the job and run into any problems or have any questions regarding the safety of your installation, don't hesitate to seek professional help.

## WORKING WITH PROFESSIONALS

Reputable stove dealers will either have their own installation crews or be able to recommend a reliable installer or general contractor to do the job. Many installers are now certified by professional organizations or have gained a limited specialized contractor's state certification to install factory-built chimney and stove systems. Brick and stone masons are likely to be experienced in hearth installation and will be able to offer custom designs in various masonry materials; or they can build a hearth to your exact specifications.

Before contracting with an installer, make sure the installer carries liability insurance. If you should have a fire and it can be traced directly to a faulty installation, the installer's insurance company will cover resulting damages.

Many installers will guarantee their work against defects in workmanship (usually for a period of 6 months to a year after installation). Under the guarantee, the installer is responsible for repairing the chimney should it leak or fall apart. Ask the installer exactly what the guarantee covers.

The installer can seldom guarantee that the chimney will draw properly because it's often difficult to determine the effect of geographical location and local weather conditions on chimney draft. An experienced installer, however,

should be familiar with these conditions and take them into account when installing the chimney.

**Getting bids.** Unless purchase price of your stove includes installation, you should attempt to get several bids on the installation work. If you're using a mason who does custom hearth work, you'll probably be getting separate bids on hearth and chimney installations.

When you get a bid, be sure you know what work and materials are included. A reputable installer will give you a bid in writing and list all materials, their prices, and a price for services performed. Because prices on materials and labor can increase, it's a good idea to find out when the bid expires and get the expiration date in writing. For instance, installers may give you a bid that's good for 30 days from date of issue, allowing you that amount of time to get competitive bids before their prices are subject to change.

Some installers work on a per-hour basis, charging you for the amount of time it takes to do the installation. If you go this route, you'll probably have to obtain the building permit and provide the necessary materials yourself. Unless the installer is insured or bonded (financially capable of accepting liability for the work), you'll be legally responsible for the safety of the installation.

**Contracts.** The agreement you make with an installer should be spelled out in a final written contract. The contract should include a complete list of materials and services, a completion date, guarantees on work and follow-up services, and a payment schedule. A good contract protects both you and the installer should either of you fail to meet its specified terms.

## DOING YOUR OWN INSTALLATION

If you want to build the chimney and hearth and install your wood stove yourself, the first task is to develop a detailed set of plans to go with your application for a building permit. Your plans should include the exact location of stove and chimney, hearth details, and a list of all hearth and chimney materials that you will need to use in the installation.

After you've presented your plans to the local building department and obtained a permit, work can begin. For most amateur builders, the easiest sequence is to install the chimney first and then build (or purchase) the hearth. This minimizes the amount of time you have a hole open to the weather.

Safety is the watchword in wood stove installation. Many destructive house fires are caused by improper installation or a faulty chimney. Make sure you're thoroughly familiar with recommended clearances (see facing page) and proper installation materials and procedures before you start, and always follow the manufacturer's directions to the letter.

## PLANNING THE INSTALLATION

Once you've purchased your stove and chosen its general location in the house, you can plan your chimney and hearth installation. Your house design and the location of your stove in the house will dictate the type of chimney you install, where you make the chimney connection, and the materials required.

You have many more choices when it comes to hearth design, however. (For some ideas shown in color, turn to pages 44–55.) Stove dealers, installers, and masons can suggest a layout or help you if you want to design your own hearth.

Installation information begins on page 104.

## STOVE & STOVEPIPE CLEARANCES

One of the prime requirements for a safe stove installation is that you place the stove and stovepipe a safe distance from all combustible materials and surfaces. In addition, you must provide adequate floor protection around the stove in the event that glowing embers or other burning materials fall from the stove. Standard clearances with and without shielding are given in the chart below.

A combustible wall or floor is one that's constructed of, or contains, a flammable material such as wood, wallboard, or vinyl. Tile is also considered a combustible material because it doesn't have adequate insular values; also, cracks in the grouting can leave openings for embers from the stove. Solid masonry walls and floors (unpainted brick,

# STANDARD STOVE & STOVEPIPE CLEARANCES

The National Fire Protection Agency (NFPA) has established the following requirements for clearances from combustibles for wood stoves and hearths. Although most local agencies have adopted these requirements, some have not. Be sure to check with your local building department before installing your wood heater to see if local requirements vary from these standards.

When shielding is used, adequate air circulation may be provided by leaving all edges of the wall protector open with at least a 1-inch air space. (You can mount the shielding on furring channels or other noncombustible spacers.) Leave a 1-inch air space from the edges of the shielding to the floor and ceiling.

All clearances are measured from the outer surface of the combustible material to the nearest point on the surface of the stove or chimney, regardless of any intervening shields.

For a look at these clearance standards and how they're affected by shielding, see the illustration that appears on page 100.

## HEARTH REQUIREMENTS

Stoves with legs providing less than 2 inches of ventilated air space to the floor must be placed on a totally noncombustible floor.

Stoves with legs providing 2 to 6 inches of ventilated air space to the floor may be placed on a combustible floor provided it's protected with 24-gauge sheet metal and one course of hollow masonry units no less than 4 inches in thickness, laid to provide air circulation.

Stoves with legs providing 6 inches or more of ventilated air space to the floor may be placed on combustible floors provided the floor is protected with 24-gauge sheet metal and solid masonry units at least 2 inches thick.

The hearth must extend at least 18 inches on all sides of the stove to unprotected walls.

## STOVE & STOVEPIPE REQUIREMENTS

**Clearances from combustibles without shielding:**

| | |
|---|---|
| Wood stove (measured from top, sides, front, and back) | 36 inches |
| Chimney connector (minimum 24-gauge single-wall stovepipe measured from sides) | 18 inches |

**Clearances from combustibles with the following shielding:**

| | Ceiling protector | Wall protector |
|---|---|---|
| 3½-inch masonry wall (no ventilated air space) | Not applicable | 24 inches |
| 3½-inch masonry wall (with ventilated air space) | Not applicable | 12 inches |
| 24-gauge sheet metal (with ventilated air space) | 18 inches | 12 inches |
| 24-gauge sheet metal over 1-inch glass fiber or mineral wool batts reinforced with wire, or equivalent, on rear face (with ventilated air space) | 18 inches | 12 inches |
| ½-inch cement board (with ventilated air space) | 18 inches | 12 inches |
| ½-inch cement board over 1-inch glass fiber or mineral wool batts (no ventilated air space) | 24 inches | 18 inches |
| 24-gauge sheet metal with ventilated air space over 24-gauge sheet metal with ventilated air space | 18 inches | 12 inches |
| 1-inch glass fiber or mineral wood batts sandwiched between 2 sheets of 24-gauge sheet metal (with ventilated air space) | 18 inches | 12 inches |

## Standard & Reduced Clearances for Wood Stoves

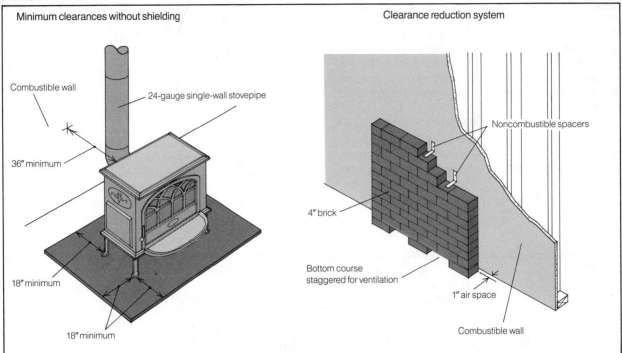

Minimum clearances without shielding

Combustible wall

24-gauge single-wall stovepipe

36" minimum

18" minimum

18" minimum

Clearance reduction system

Noncombustible spacers

4" brick

Bottom course staggered for ventilation

1" air space

Combustible wall

stone, or concrete) are considered noncombustible unless they're covered with a combustible material, such as wallpaper, wood, or carpeting.

**Clearance standards.** The National Fire Protection Association (NFPA) recommends minimum safe clearances and installation standards for wood stoves (see "Standard Stove & Stovepipe Clearances" on page 99). These standards have been adopted by most building departments across the country and by the stove industry as a whole. Today's wood stoves have been safety-tested and listed by nationally certified testing laboratories, and bear permanent labels with clearance and hearth requirements.

The NFPA recommends that wood stoves be at least 36 inches away from combustible walls and ceilings. However, always check the manufacturer's specifications, since your stove may have a different clearance listing.

**Reducing clearance requirements.** Most stoves today have been tested for reduced clearances to combustibles accomplished through the use of stove and pipe shields or double-wall chimney connectors. If a stove manufacturer using these techniques successfully safety-tests its stoves for reduced clearances, those clearances may be applied and will pass building department inspections.

To reduce stove clearances to a combustible wall, you need to protect the surface with a noncombustible material—3½-inch-thick masonry, 24-gauge sheet metal, or ½-inch-thick cement board (see page 99). All must be installed with spacers to maintain a 1-inch ventilated air space between the combustible wall and the shield.

**Clearance for the chimney connection.** In addition to stove and stovepipe clearances, you must also allow adequate clearance where the chimney connector meets the chimney. At this point, an insulated chimney support assembly or insulated pipe fitting is used to protect the wall or ceiling, as explained on page 103.

## DETERMINING STOVE PLACEMENT

One of the most important factors to consider when you're planning the precise location of your stove is the clearance required for the stove and stovepipe from combustible surfaces (for clearance standards, see page 99). Another is the best location for the chimney outlet in the room.

Keep in mind that the chimney and chimney connection should be as vertical as possible, minimizing horizontal runs, bends, or offsets that restrict draft. (The *chimney connection* includes all components used inside the stove room to connect the stove to the chimney. The *chimney* includes all pipe, masonry, and other permanent components used to vent the smoke outdoors.)

If you're installing a new chimney, you'll first need to decide where the chimney will run, as explained on the facing page; then you can locate the chimney opening in the wall or ceiling as close as possible to the intended stove position.

If you're venting the stove into an existing fireplace or unused chimney, the placement of the stove will be restricted by the location of the chimney or fireplace opening.

A stove should never be placed in a closet or alcove, unless the stove has been specifically tested for that placement by the manufacturer. Some newer models are now made for alcoves.

## LOCATING THE CHIMNEY CONNECTION & CHIMNEY

Typically, wood stoves are vented through prefabricated metal chimneys installed for that purpose. A more expensive and difficult alternative is to build a masonry fireplace and chimney made of brick, concrete blocks, or stone, with special flue tile liners (for a detailed look at masonry fireplaces, turn to pages 77–83).

If you want to use an existing masonry chimney or flue, several precautions must be taken in order to promote efficient draft and reduce the danger of a chimney fire. For information on using an existing chimney, see page 106.

When you're determining the path the chimney and chimney connection will take, remember that the chimney should be as vertical as possible, avoiding any obstructions, such as studs, joists, or other framing members. Several chimney installations are shown on page 102; refer to the illustration to determine which one best suits the intended location of your stove. Your stove dealer or chimney supply outlet can help you estimate the amount of materials you'll need.

**Chimney connection.** In planning the location of the chimney connection, you'll need to know the position of the stove within the location you've chosen for it. To position the stove, find out the stove's dimensions and the location of its flue vent where the stovepipe is attached. If you already have the stove and it's light enough to jockey around easily, you can set it in its intended position, allowing the proper clearances to the wall. Otherwise, make a scale drawing of the stove, its position in the room, and the location of the flue vent.

To plot the path the chimney connection will take, mark the location on the wall or ceiling where the chimney connection will join the outside chimney. Here, you'll have to cut a hole through the wall or ceiling large enough to accept the chimney support assembly. (For a look at the installation procedure, see Step 2 on page 104.)

Ideally, the opening in the wall or ceiling should be centered between the studs or joists. To locate them, use a stud sensor, tap on the wall (listen for a solid thud), or measure from a nearby door or window (studs are usually set 16 or 24 inches on center). If the support assembly is too large to fit between the studs or joists, you'll have to cut one of them and frame in the correct size opening.

Mark the size of the intended hole on the wall or ceiling and find its center point. Then align the center point of the stove's flue vent to the center point of the marked opening. Recheck clearances—if the stove no longer meets the required clearances once it's aligned with the chimney opening, either offset the chimney connection or relocate the opening to provide the necessary clearance.

**Chimney.** To determine the run of the outside chimney, find and mark (with a nail or by drilling a hole through the

wall or ceiling) the location of the opening on the outside of the wall or other side of the ceiling. If the chimney will be running through an attic or second story, make sure there are no obstructions directly above the intended opening. To determine the approximate location of the roof opening, drop a plumb bob and align it with the ceiling opening.

The chimney run should be as vertical as possible; if you find a rafter or other framing member in the way of the chimney, you'll have to offset the pipe to avoid it (or adjust the opening).

## DESIGNING THE HEARTH

Planning the hearth involves deciding what material to use and determining the exact dimensions necessary to provide adequate clearance to combustibles.

**Materials.** Hearths for wood stoves can be made of brick, stone, metal, or any other noncombustible material. Some hearths even come ready-made from the factory. Many wood stove outlets offer factory-built hearths that can be set directly on the floor.

Stove hearths are designed to protect the floor from the heat of the stove. Extending the protection up the wall isn't necessary if proper clearances to combustibles are maintained, although you may wish to for purely esthetic

### A Typical Hearth Design

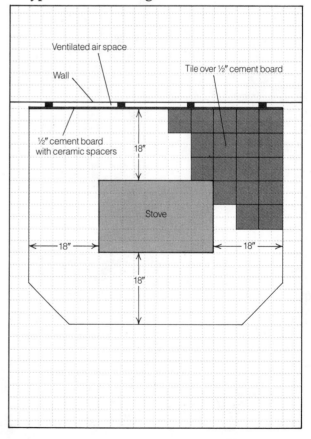

Ventilated air space

Wall

Tile over ½" cement board

½" cement board with ceramic spacers

18"

Stove

18"

18"

18"

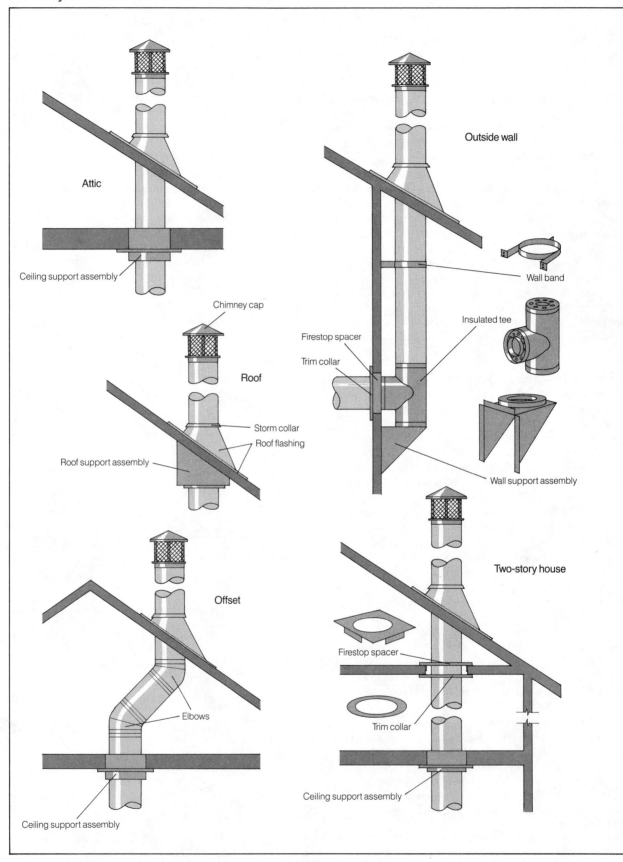

Attic

Ceiling support assembly

Chimney cap

Roof

Storm collar

Roof flashing

Roof support assembly

Offset

Elbows

Ceiling support assembly

Outside wall

Wall band

Insulated tee

Firestop spacer

Trim collar

Wall support assembly

Two-story house

Firestop spacer

Trim collar

Ceiling support assembly

reasons. If you want to reduce the minimum clearances to the wall and floor safely, you must first provide the protection prescribed by your local building department before you apply the covering materials.

**Dimensions.** Hearth size is governed by clearance requirements. Consult the information on page 99 and the manufacturer's specifications for guidelines.

In planning your hearth, you may want to draw it and the location of the stove on graph paper. This drawing can help you figure hearth materials. (For a look at a typical hearth design, see page 101.)

## COMPONENTS FOR A PREFABRICATED METAL CHIMNEY

Chimney installation is done in two parts: the chimney itself and all components in the stove room making up the chimney connection. Unlike a built-in fireplace, where the chimney is supported by the fireplace, the chimney of a wood stove is supported by the wall or ceiling where it exits the room. In addition to standard components, the installation will require a chimney support system, which includes all the pieces required to support the weight of the chimney.

**Choosing the right pipe.** Chimneys for wood stoves must be insulated to keep smoke and flue gases hot enough to rise up the chimney. If the flue gases cool in the chimney, the stove won't draw efficiently, resulting in "backpuffing" of smoke through the stove and excess creosote buildup caused by condensation of gases inside the chimney.

Pipes and fittings for prefabricated metal chimneys must be approved by Underwriter's Laboratories (UL) and by local codes. Several kinds of insulated and ventilated double- and triple-wall stainless steel pipe are approved for wood stove chimneys. Don't make the mistake of using single-wall pipe or vent pipe intended for gas furnaces and water heaters, even in a second-story room. These pipes are not allowed for use with wood stoves and can lead to costly and dangerous chimney fires.

Insulated pipes use insulation to block heat from escaping the chimney; ventilated pipes use thermo-siphoned air to circulate and cool between pipe walls. Some pipes now come both insulated and ventilated. One type is shown above, at right.

**Other chimney components.** Because houses are different and there are usually several possible locations for chimneys in any house, there are numerous prefabricated metal chimney components and fittings for different situations. Standard components for all factory-built chimneys include a chimney support assembly, roof flashing, a storm collar, and a chimney termination cap. Other necessary components will depend on the particular chimney installation.

Support assemblies are available for wall-supported chimneys, for chimneys supported by rafters in the roof, and for those supported by joists in the ceiling. Wall support assemblies include brackets and a plate that are at-

## Metal Chimney Pipe

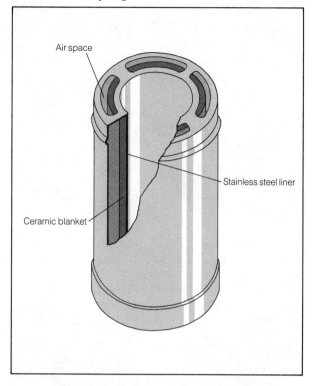

*Insulated and ventilated stainless steel pipe makes a firesafe chimney for a wood stove.*

tached to the outside wall to support the chimney. To connect a wall-supported chimney to the stovepipe inside, you'll need an insulated tee so the chimney will pass safely through the wall. Roof and ceiling chimney supports should be equipped with noncombustible firestop spacers so they'll pass safely through combustible roofs and ceilings.

If you're running the chimney through a second-story room or finished attic, you'll need a pair of support units for the first ceiling the chimney passes through and a firestop spacer for the second-story ceiling and roof. Ask your stove dealer which type of support unit will best fit your situation.

Other components you'll need include wall bands and metal braces to laterally reinforce the chimney up an outside wall and above the roof, and a variety of trim and finishing collars to cover holes where the chimney passes through walls or ceilings. Common chimney installations and their components are illustrated on the facing page.

A knowledgeable stove dealer can help you choose the necessary components for your installation and provide you with the materials you need. When figuring how much pipe you need for the chimney and chimney connection, add an extra length or two to be on the safe side.

Manufacturers of prefabricated metal chimneys usually provide detailed installation instructions that will tell you how to estimate your material requirements. When you're measuring, remember that chimney pipe sections overlap when assembled, so you'll lose an inch or two from each measured pipe length.

**Step 1**

Opening for chimney support system

**Step 2 (for ceiling- or roof-supported chimney)**

Chimney support box

**Step 3a (for ceiling- or roof-supported chimney)**

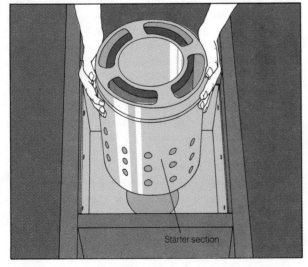

Starter section

## INSTALLING THE CHIMNEY & HEARTH

Three things are a *must* for a safe stove installation: proper materials, adequate clearance, and proper assembly of all components.

Faulty chimney installations cause many stove-related fires. Take extra care in this phase of your stove installation. If the chimney is not installed in strict accordance with the manufacturer's instructions, your insurance company may not pay for damages resulting from a chimney fire.

Because each chimney installation is slightly different, you're likely to encounter a few unique problems when you install yours. If you're having difficulty with your installation, don't hesitate to seek professional advice from a stove installer or general contractor familiar with stove installation.

Below is a general guide to the installation procedure.

**Step 1. Locating and cutting the opening.** Determine where the chimney will enter the wall or ceiling and cut a hole between the wall studs or ceiling joists for the support assembly. (Turn off the electricity to the house in case you run into any wires while you're cutting.) If the support assembly, firestop spacer, or thimble won't fit between the studs or joists, you'll have to frame the opening in the same way that you frame in for a firestop spacer above a built-in fireplace (see Steps 3 and 4 on page 88).

Then cut the outside hole and attach nailing blocks between the studs or joists to fit the support assembly.

If you're cutting holes in both the ceiling and roof, cut the ceiling hole first; then, using a plumb bob, you can align the ceiling hole with the proposed roof hole. You may have to offset the chimney pipe slightly with a pair of elbows to center the roof support assembly between the roof rafters or to pass pipes closer to the roof ridge. If you cannot avoid trimming a rafter, be sure to add adequate support framing (see Steps 6 and 7 on page 89).

**Step 2. Installing the support assembly.** Following the manufacturer's directions, add the ceiling or roof support box and remaining components. For wall-supported chimneys, the support assembly consists of an insulated tee, a firestop spacer, and a support bracket. An insulated pipe attaches to the tee and passes through the wall, ending a minimum of 4 inches beyond the inside wall surface.

Typical support assemblies are illustrated on page 102.

**Step 3. Assembling the chimney sections.** Before you begin installing the chimney pipe sections, practice fitting pipe sections together. Insulated chimney pipe sections are interlocking. Some types use slip rings to lock the sections together; others are simply fitted together and twisted to lock them in place. Sections are usually marked with an arrow or the word "up" to orient you.

Once the starter section of pipe is fitted into the support assembly, attach any fittings by slipping them into position over the pipe before attaching additional lengths of pipe.

*For a roof- or ceiling-supported chimney,* fit the starter section into the support box, as shown in Step 3a, and continue fitting pipe sections together. To finish the installation on the roof, follow Steps 8 and 9 on page 89.

*For a wall-supported chimney,* you'll have to extend the chimney sections through the eave or bypass it, depending on the width of the eave. If the eave is wide enough, the simplest and easiest method is to cut through it, using supports for the chimney.

If the eave is too narrow for this, you have two options. In cases where the roof overhang is narrower than the outside diameter of the pipe, you can block out the tee and add longer horizontal pipe to set the chimney far enough away from the wall to clear the eave by 2 inches; spacer blocks attached to the wall anchor the wall bands, as shown in Step 3b. But if the roof overhang is as wide as or wider than the outside diameter of the pipe, use 15° elbows to offset the chimney.

In both cases, the section above the eave line must be supported and braced as shown.

**Step 4. Building the hearth.** Floor hearths are fairly simple to build. Typically, you lay down ½-inch-thick cement board and bond tile, brick, or other masonry to it. Then you grout the joints.

Extending a masonry shield up the wall is more difficult, especially if it requires wall protection behind it. You'll need considerable experience for most of these types of installations.

If your hearth or its extension is fairly complicated, get help from an experienced mason or stove installer.

**Step 5. Making the chimney connection.** Carefully position the stove on the hearth prepared for it. If you use single-wall black stovepipe to connect the stove to the chimney opening, it should be at least 24 gauge. Don't use aluminum or galvanized pipe.

Stovepipe comes in 6-, 7-, and 8-inch diameters to fit all American-made stoves. If possible, the diameter of the stovepipe should be the same size as the flue opening in the stove.

Make the chimney connection as short and direct as possible—a straight vertical run of pipe from the stove to the ceiling or a short horizontal run of pipe from the back of the stove to a chimney opening directly behind it.

Try to avoid having more than one 90° elbow for the chimney connection. If your connection requires a bend less than 90°, buy an adjustable elbow that will make bends up to 90°. Some stoves may require the use of a flue damper to control the draft; install it in the first section of the stovepipe 6 to 12 inches above the flue collar of the stove.

Stovepipe generally has one crimped end with a slightly smaller diameter so the pipes will fit together.

**Step 3b (for wall-supported chimney)**

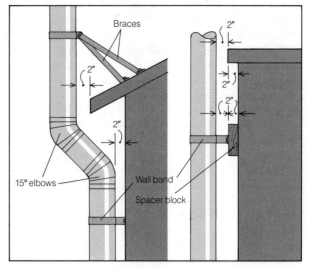

**Step 4**

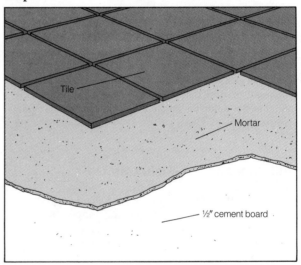

**Step 5**

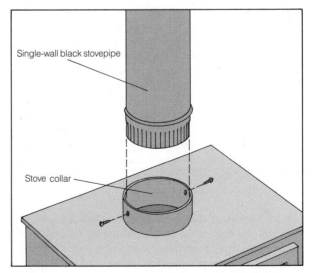

Assemble the pipes crimped ends down so creosote won't leak through the joints. If the pipe doesn't fit the collar on your stove, you'll have to use a flue adapter or have a bushing specially made for your stove. Fasten sections together with sheet-metal screws; prefabricated stovepipe fastens by a twist-and-lock motion.

Support horizontal runs of pipe every 2 feet (runs should rarely be longer than that anyway); support vertical pipe at least every 6 feet. Be sure all pipe and fittings have the required 18-inch clearance from combustible surfaces (see the clearance guidelines on page 99).

If you need to cut any lengths of pipe, be careful not to bend the pipe out of shape when cutting. Slip adapters can help you eliminate unnecessary cutting. Most prefabricated chimney manufacturers have flue connection kits which include enough interlocking pipe and necessary components to do a single installation.

The final length of stovepipe connects to the chimney support assembly or insulated chimney fitting in the wall or ceiling.

**Step 6. Checking the work.** Once your stove is connected to the chimney and the installation is complete, go back and check the entire chimney and chimney connection, inch by inch. Make sure all joints and other components are fastened securely. Next, light a small, smoky fire in the stove, using damp leaves or newspaper, and check the chimney again for smoke leaks. Make any final repairs necessary.

## RELINING AN EXISTING CHIMNEY

Venting any type of wood-burning appliance, especially the newer wood stoves with their high-temperature emissions, into an existing chimney that isn't modified can severely reduce the efficiency of the wood heater and can easily cause a chimney fire.

The problem is that many existing chimneys, especially masonry ones, have too large a flue to provide optimum efficiency for today's wood stoves. Moreover, the flues are often in poor condition.

The best solution is to reline your chimney, using one of the techniques described in this section. Relining your chimney will help create a better draft, making your wood heater more efficient, and the hotter flue temperatures will help minimize the buildup of creosote, thus minimizing the chance of a chimney fire. (The majority of chimney fires today are caused by wood burners connected to unmodified masonry chimneys.)

Keep in mind also that your existing hearth must meet the clearance requirements specified by your wood stove manufacturer. If it doesn't, you'll have to adapt it as well.

**Inspecting your chimney.** If you have an existing chimney that you want to use, have it thoroughly checked by a professional mason, chimney sweep, or member of your local fire department for defects and creosote buildup, prior to installing your stove. If the chimney needs repairs, first get an estimate from a mason. You may find it will cost more to repair the old chimney than to install a new one.

Specifically, check to see that the chimney opening in the room (the thimble) and the chimney's inside flue diameter are the same size or larger than the diameter of the stove's flue connection. The thimble must be made of galvanized steel with a minimum thickness of 24 gauge or of a material of equivalent durability; it should also meet current NFPA standards. If the chimney opening does not have a thimble or it's the wrong size, you'll have to install one.

**Relining techniques.** You can reline your existing chimney by adding a rigid or flexible stainless steel insert surrounded by nonflammable insulation (shown below), by pouring in thermal concrete with insulation mixed into the mortar, or by installing a stainless steel pipe wrapped with insulation.

Some home owners adding stainless steel pipes to their existing chimneys extend them just past the first flue liner and seal them below the damper plate. Although this practice may be allowed, it makes the chimney very difficult to clean. NFPA guidelines state that the existing fireplace flue must be not more than three times larger than the stove collar. Flues that are too large will stay relatively cool, collecting creosote, and they'll restrict draft to the wood stove.

### Relining a Chimney

*To reline an existing masonry chimney, use a stainless steel liner surrounded by nonflammable insulation.*

# WOOD STOVE SAFETY, MAINTENANCE & USE

Most longtime wood stove users agree that the cozy heat of their stoves more than repays the effort that goes into producing it, but it does require effort. Wood stoves, with the possible exception of the new pellet stoves, are not automatic appliances; most require a break-in period, both of stove and stove owner.

## FIRING THE STOVE

Safety, fire management, ash removal, and maintenance techniques are largely matters of common sense and experience and are not difficult to master. Yet each is extremely important both to your enjoyment of your wood stove and to its safe and efficient operation. Investing a little time in the care and feeding of your stove will repay you many times over.

## SAFETY FIRST!

The operation of a wood stove can be quite safe and convenient, but its very convenience can lead you to relax your vigilance. Be sure never to lose sight of the fact that there's a box with a fire in it in your house.

Here are some important tips for safe operation of your wood stove:

■ *Burn only well-seasoned hardwoods, if possible.* Softwoods are best for kindling and for mixing occasionally with hardwoods to increase the intensity of the fire. Most softwoods smoke, make sparks, and form creosote much faster than hardwoods do. Never burn green (unseasoned) wood of any kind.

■ *Use a chimney thermometer* to measure the temperature inside the stove. This prevents overfiring the stove or running it too low, allowing creosote to build up. Ask your dealer for recommended temperatures.

■ *Never use any sort of flammable liquid* to start or encourage the fire—not even charcoal lighter fluid. Using these liquids in the enclosed firebox of a stove can produce an explosion.

■ *Keep combustibles at least 3 feet away from the stove.* It's easy to misjudge the power of radiated heat, since it doesn't heat the air. A hot stove is a remarkably effective fire starter when combustibles are too close.

■ *Exercise extreme caution any time the door is open*— embers may be still present and can pop out even when the fire appears to be dead. When you open the door, do so slowly to bleed air in gradually.

■ *Never burn trash in your stove.* The fast, hot fire from the trash will abuse the stove and flue. For the same reason, sawdust logs and chemical logs should never be used; they burn too hot.

## BUILDING THE FIRE

Once your stove is installed, make a small test fire; the idea is to create enough smoke to check the tightness of all seams and connections without committing yourself to an hours-long blaze. The test fire can be nothing more than a few sheets of newspaper, perhaps with some wet leaves to ensure enough smoke. Be sure all dampers are open before you light the fire, and make sure you have followed all of the manufacturer's instructions for preparing the stove. Once your installation checks out, you're ready to begin in earnest.

Most stoves need to be broken in, or seasoned. To do this, make the first few fires small and avoid sudden bursts of heat. At first, condensation will occur on the stove; wipe it away continuously so it doesn't stain the surface. If your stove is painted, it may "smell funny" at first; this is only the oil in the paint evaporating and will stop after the first few fires.

To build a fire, crumple newspaper into balls and distribute them over the bottom of the firebox (see illustration below). Follow these with dry kindling, such as dry soft-

### Building a Fire

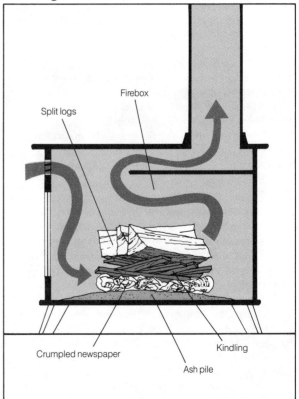

*To lay a fire in a wood stove, start with newspaper; then top with kindling and split logs.*

wood or lumber scraps, about ½ to 1 inch in diameter. Allowing air passages between the sticks, lay the kindling in a crisscross fashion, making sure the sticks are close enough to allow fire to spread from one to the other. Remember that a fire needs heat, oxygen, and fuel to burn; packing kindling too tightly will exclude oxygen from the fire. In fact, this is probably the most common cause of failure in fire building.

Then add several pieces of dry, seasoned hardwood, progressing from smaller to larger pieces. Again, air needs to be able to circulate around the splits, but they need to be close enough to "feed" each other once they're burning.

Check that the flue damper is open and that the stove draft controls are set for maximum draft. Light the newspaper and immediately close the door. Don't be tempted to have a look to see the logs start burning; they'll do much better with the regulated draft provided by the stove's controls than they will with the excess air flowing through the door.

If your first attempt fails, try again with fresh kindling and paper. If your kindling is dry, patience and persistence will be rewarded. In fact, once you've learned your stove's fire-starting idiosyncrasies, you'll probably find it easier to light than a fireplace or a camp fire.

## MANAGING THE FIRE

Trial and error will be your guides once the fire is burning. Stoves differ in the amount of fuel they need, and the size of your house and the rate of firing will have an effect on your fire.

**Temperature control.** The heat output of your stove is governed by the size of the fire, which, in turn, is governed by the damper and air inlet settings as well as the amount of fuel in the firebox. Generally, the more air that passes through the stove, the hotter the fire will burn—as long as it's supplied with fuel. To slow the fire, turn down the inlet drafts, the damper, or both. Better yet, refrain from overstoking the firebox.

A common complaint—or boast—of wood stove owners is that their stoves drive them out of the house with heat. This can be prevented by first choosing a stove with the correct heating capacity for your situation. Don't be deceived by the relatively small size of most stoves; they're quite powerful if fired at their maximum rate. Yet, this is what you should try to do, at least part of the time, to keep the flue clean. Strive to regulate the heat output of your stove by adjusting the amount of fuel you add, not by constantly damping down the fire. If your stove is not oversized for your situation, this should be possible.

**Reloading.** When you reload your stove, it's a good idea to open the draft controls and damper before opening the door. This will help prevent backpuffing of smoke into the room. Also, wait until the chimney is warm and the draft well established before you refuel the stove.

After reloading, run the stove with dampers and inlets open for about half an hour to help retard the formation of creosote, most of which is given off in the early stages of firing. The best time to damp down your stove is after the fire has reached the coaling stage and most of the wood has been consumed.

**Banking the fire.** To make it easier to start the fire each day, bank your fire the previous night by raking the last of the evening's coals and embers into the center of the stove. Cover them with ashes and close the draft controls to minimum setting. A thick layer of ashes will exclude most air from the coals and prevent their burning up during the night. Uncover them in the morning, rake them to the front of the stove, and place several pieces of firewood on top. Close the door, open the drafts all the way, and in a few minutes your morning's fire will be burning.

**Overnight burning.** In the past, overnight burning caused a serious creosote problem because the older stoves emitted large amounts of creosote and soot when they weren't burned to capacity.

By law, modern stoves must burn at least five times cleaner than the stoves of the 1970's, so low-damper, overnight burning doesn't cause as much of a creosote problem as it did years ago.

If you want to hold a fire overnight, place one or two large logs on a good bed of coals, operate the stove at full draft until the wood is well ignited, and then reset the inlet draft controls so you have a flame height of a few inches. The temperature of the surface of the stove and the flue exhaust should be between 500°F/260°C and 600°F/315°C. (Use a chimney thermometer to measure the temperature.)

## STOVE & FLUE MAINTENANCE

Regular attention paid to your stove and flue will pay you back in increased heating efficiency and in the security of knowing your wood-heating system is safe. Most stoves need little maintenance; beyond a regular cleaning, neither does a quality chimney installation.

### KEEPING THE INTERIOR CLEAN

Because of their highly efficient burning characteristics, wood stoves on the market today present fewer problems with ash accumulation and creosote buildup than older models. Still, these are problems you'll have to attend to periodically.

**Ashes.** Eventually, of course, ashes will build up in every stove, including pellet stoves, and will have to be removed.

A stove with a built-in ash pan need not be emptied until the pan is full; in fact, a layer of ashes in any stove will help encourage the fire—it acts as an insulator, holding the heat in the coals at the bottom of the fire. For help with ash removal, see page 96.

**Creosote.** The biggest enemy of the interior of your flue and chimney is creosote (see page 94). In the past, creosote was a significant problem with the older, so-called airtight stoves, but stoves that meet current government emission standards emit far less creosote, even at low draft settings.

If the flue temperature falls much below 300°F/149°C, creosote deposits will begin to form. To keep the flue heated properly, try to run your stove at its capacity as often as possible. If you plan to run it at a low setting overnight, for example, be sure to burn it at capacity for 20 or 30 minutes first to evaporate the creosote-causing moisture in the wood. Then you can reduce the air intake. First thing in the morning, open the air control again and let the stove burn hot to burn off any creosote built up the night before.

But even the highly sophisticated modern stoves will, sooner or later, cause creosote buildup in the chimney, so regular cleaning will still be necessary. Inspect your chimney and connecting pipes regularly. Plan to clean the flue at least once a year, more often if the stove is in daily use—especially if you burn it overnight at low settings. Creosote is part of wood heat, but it need not be a hazard. For information on cleaning your chimney and flue, see page 96.

## STOVE UPKEEP

The need for maintenance increases in proportion to stove use. If yours is a hard worker, one that's fired daily through the heating season, plan to check it at least once a month. Then it will continue to work hard for you in years to come.

**Surface.** To maintain a painted surface, you'll need to perform a yearly retouching with a high-temperature paint or stove polish. This prevents rusting and hides the chalking that occurs on most matte-surfaced stoves. Porcelain enamel surfaces, although delicate and somewhat expensive, need only an occasional wiping with a damp sponge.

**Firebox.** Check the grates and burn plates, if any, for burnout. These parts are subject to considerable heat stress and will eventually become oxidized and need replacement. Be sure the firebox is adequately protected by sand or ashes if it has no grate. Clean inner walls with a wire brush.

**Doors.** The gaskets used to seal the doors on many stoves will need replacement every few years. Your dealer should be able to supply you with new ones.

**Seams.** Cast-iron stoves with seams sealed by furnace cement should be carefully checked. The cement eventually dries out and becomes brittle. Unless seams are very tight, the cement may eventually fall out. Then you'll have to rebuild the stove.

## WOOD STORAGE IDEAS

Corralling an unruly woodpile in an outside shelter or frame that has a raised floor allows the wood to dry faster, re-duces the possibility of insect infestation, and keeps the wood from rotting. A neat woodpile also looks better and allows the wood to dry evenly. A good wood shelter can even work as a solar dryer, allowing the sun and wind to enter during the summer and blocking the rain in the winter.

There are a number of designs you can use for your woodpile shelter. Three examples are described and illustrated below. (For wood storage ideas you can use inside your house, glance through the chapter that begins on page 15.)

**End frames.** One easy-to-make frame that can be used on almost any size woodpile works on the same principle as expandable bookends. The weight of the logs anchors the frames at the ends of the stack. As the stack grows or diminishes, you just move the end frames closer together or farther apart to accommodate it.

Make two end frames out of 2 by 4s. Don't lay the logs between the end frames directly on the ground; instead, set them on redwood or cedar runners between the frames.

**Covered woodshed.** You can shelter your wood from rain by building a simple cedar or pressure-treated wood frame and covering it with plywood. Make the floor of wood slats so that any moisture that might leak in can find its way out again. You can connect the shed to the house wall, utilizing it for support and to enclose the back of the woodshed, but if your wood is infested with insects, they can attack the house wall.

**Freestanding wood shelter.** The freestanding firewood shelter shown below loads from either side. It's easy to build from standard lumber and plywood. Where the wood is in direct contact with the ground, be sure to use only decay-resistant cypress or cedar heartwood, or pressure-treated lumber. For full stability, this shelter requires at least a partial load of wood.

### Three Ways to Store Wood

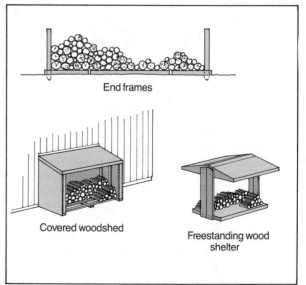

End frames

Covered woodshed

Freestanding wood shelter

# WOODCHOPPER'S GUIDE

Heating with wood, unlike most conventional heating methods, means that you'll need to find and often transport your own supply of fuel. First, you must decide which wood species in your area make the best firewood; then you'll have to locate a source, bring the wood home, and prepare it—cut, stacked, and seasoned—to feed your fire.

## HOW TO CHOOSE WOOD

The wood you burn in your stove or fireplace must be well seasoned. Beyond that, your choices will be limited by availability—remember that not all wood species are available everywhere—and price.

## HARDWOODS OR SOFTWOODS?

All wood is divided into two categories, hardwoods and softwoods, terms that refer to the origin of the wood. Hardwoods come from broad-leafed, usually deciduous trees, which include oak, hickory, and maple. Softwoods are the conifers, or evergreens, such as pine, fir, and cedar. Pound for pound, all woods have about the same heating value, but because hardwoods are more dense, they yield more heat by volume.

Hardwoods are generally denser and less resinous than softwoods; thus, they burn more slowly, producing a more even heat. Softwoods burn hot and fast, making them excellent for kindling, but if you use them as your primary fuel, you'll be feeding the stove very often. Softwoods also produce more creosote (see page 94) than hardwoods, which means more frequent flue cleaning. For a hot, even fire, it's best to burn a mix of about 80 percent hardwoods and 20 percent softwoods. One excellent combination is oak and cedar.

Heat values aside, wood species within the two major categories have individual characteristics you'll have to consider. For instance, straight-grained woods, such as birch and red oak, are easier to split than woods with spiral or intertwined grain patterns. Ironwood and hardhack have earned their names well, judging from the number of saw blades and ax bits dulled in cutting. Some woods, including many softwoods, are heavy smoke-producers; others contain moisture pockets which cause them to snap and pop, so they throw off sparks as they burn. Many fruitwoods, such as apple, burn with a pleasant fragrance. For a chart showing some of the most important characteristics of the various wood species, turn to page 9.

Experienced wood-burners in your area will obligingly advise you on the burning qualities of indigenous woods. They'll probably agree that the best choices, overall, are ash, beech, birch, hickory, oak (all species), and hard maple. They all have high heat values, burn well, produce little smoke, and split fairly easily.

## SEASONED WOOD

One of the most frequent mistakes wood-burners make is trying to burn green, or unseasoned, wood. More than half the weight of freshly cut, green wood is water. It takes at least 9 months to season wood; it's best to give wood at least 2 years to season, if possible.

Seasoned wood will lose more than 60 percent of its moisture and, therefore, will yield much more heat when burned. It's also much lighter to handle.

When buying wood, you may not be able to tell how long it's been seasoned, but you can tell if it's freshly cut. The interior of a freshly cut log, when split, will actually feel damp to your hand and will be darker than the exterior. It will also be much heavier than a similarly sized dry log. Sometimes, large cracks on the end of the log indicate that it's been seasoned. But to make sure, buy or cut your firewood in the spring, then stack it and let it season all summer, or longer, if possible.

## FROM TREE TO FIRE

Whether you prefer to buy your wood already cut and trimmed or you'll settle for nothing less than felling a tree yourself and chopping it into firewood, you'll need to locate a supply of wood adequate for your needs.

## FINDING FIREWOOD

If you simply want to buy wood that's already cut and split, the Yellow Pages and the classified ad section of your local newspaper are two good places to find firewood for sale. Be sure to check the wood before you buy. Firewood is sold by the cord—a stack of wood 4 feet high by 4 feet wide by 8 feet long. Measure it before you buy and make sure it's stacked tightly.

Most firewood outlets will deliver the wood to your house, if you don't live too far away. However, they'll charge for delivery and generally won't stack it for you at your home.

If you're willing to cut and haul your own wood, there's a variety of potential sources you can investigate for free, or almost free, firewood. The quality of the wood will vary, from softwood kindling, such as lumber scraps from construction sites, to substantial hardwood logs. Of course, urban dwellers will find their possibilities more limited than people who live in suburban and rural areas.

You'll need a truck or trailer capable of transporting a good-size load of wood, especially if you have to travel any distance to get it. You'll also need tools, including a chain saw, ax, and other cutting and splitting tools.

Here are some suggestions of places where you may find free or low-cost wood.

■ *Construction sites.* Building, remodeling, or demolition always results in some scrap, mostly short bits of pine or fir dimension lumber. In most cases, the contractor, when asked, will let you remove the leftovers.

■ *Parks.* Park maintenance includes trimming trees and felling dead or diseased trees. A check with your local department may turn up several sources of wood. This is one of the best opportunities for city dwellers to obtain choice hardwoods for burning. Remember, however, that the wood will most likely require seasoning.

■ *Utility companies.* Electric and telephone rights of way require constant maintenance. Utility crews trim branches regularly to keep them from interfering with wires; often, the wood is available for the taking. Call your local utilities' offices for permission and information on current work sites.

■ *Large landholdings.* Many farmers and ranchers have more downed wood than they can use themselves. Sometimes, they must remove trees to accommodate expanded plantings; other times, they have to thin orchards of dead trees or remove them entirely. They may welcome your offer to remove wood. Even timber companies usually leave a good deal of unsalable timber on their property after a logging operation.

■ *State and national forests.* Forest conservation requires periodic thinning of dead and diseased trees and removal of downed wood. Most state and national forestry services have programs that allow wood removal by private individuals. If you're fortunate enough to live near a state or national forest, contact your local forestry service for details on designated wood removal areas. You'll most likely have to secure a permit and perhaps pay a token fee for the wood you take.

Take only dead or downed wood. In most state and national forests, it's against the law to cut living trees, or trees marked as a wildlife habitat.

## LIMBING & BUCKING WOOD

Limbing, that is cutting off the branches from the trunk, and bucking, sawing the tree into stove-length sections, should be done at the site to avoid getting sawdust all over your own property and to make the logs easier to haul. Be sure to measure and mark each section to your stove or fireplace size before you buck the tree.

You'll need a chain saw, unless you're cutting only a few pieces. Chain saws can be very dangerous if not used properly, so be sure you follow the manufacturer's advice on use and maintenance. Wear gloves to protect your hands from splinters and cuts, and always wear goggles when cutting wood.

## SPLITTING WOOD

Plan to split all logs more than 6 inches in diameter for faster seasoning. When splitting, use an anchored chop-ping block or a stump larger in diameter than the largest piece of wood to be split. Splitting pieces on the ground is not a good idea, because the ground absorbs much of the energy of your swing, and the dirt will quickly dull your ax or maul.

Relatively small pieces for kindling may be split with a hatchet; for medium-size to large pieces, use a 6- to 10-pound maul. Extremely large or difficult-to-split pieces may require the use of two or more metal wedges and a sledgehammer, or the blunt end of a maul.

Be sure to inspect your wedges and maul before splitting. If the head of the wedge is beginning to mushroom, be sure to file off the flattened sections; otherwise, they can splinter off and become dangerous flying missiles.

Look for cracks at the end of the logs—these usually provide a head start on a clean split. If you get a maul or wedge stuck in a log, pound another wedge into the far side of the crack until the maul or wedge comes free. Split large pieces away at the edges; then split through the remaining chunk.

## STACKING & SEASONING FIREWOOD

Once the wood is cut and split into stove-size pieces, it must be stacked and stored for seasoning.

For wood to season properly, store it off the ground on concrete blocks or old pieces of lumber and keep it under cover during wet periods. It's best not to stack your wood against the wall of your house. Firewood is often host to termites and other harmful pests that can infest your home.

There are two stacking methods: parallel and crisscross (see below). A good way to build a wood pile is to use the crisscross method for the end stacks and then fill wood in between using the parallel method. With either method, pieces with bark should be placed on top, bark side up, since bark repels water better than interior wood.

### Two Methods of Stacking Firewood

*You can stack wood two ways—parallel (at left) saves space, crisscross (at right) speeds drying.*

# INDEX